NEVER WAIT FOR THE FIRE TRUCK

How the world's deadliest plane crash changed my life and yours.

David Yeager Alexander

Survivor, 1977 plane crash at Tenerife, Canary Islands

with

Diane Nelson Abel, Editor

William G. Winquist,
Captain, Retired, United Airlines

Designed by Gwyn Smith

Library of Congress Control Number: 2015911496

CreateSpace Independent Publishing Platform, North Charleston, SC

ISBN-13 978-0692471876

BISAC: B10006000

FOR

I want to thank my special friend and sailing companion, Tina Sunderland, for her encouragement to start and continue with this writing project. She is a unique woman in that she really enjoys sailing and being out on the water. Her family was always involved in sailing, whether on a lake or on San Francisco Bay. After she became single again, she spent more time on her father's sailboat, a Cal 29 named "VASA V", named after the famous Swedish Navy vessel that sank on her maiden voyage in Stockholm harbor on August 10, 1628. I have been a water person for a long time and she is too. We love being out on the San Francisco Bay on board my Catalina 30 sailboat, JAMAICA 3. This is my third boat and this one is named after my favorite destination.

Over time a number of people have suggested that I write a book about my experiences surrounding the Canary Islands aircraft accident. I was finally ready to start writing in the fall of 2011. Thanks to all of you for your support.

CONTENTS

ACKNOWLEDGEMENTS

It is amazing how events work out for the best at times. A couple joined my yacht club (Ballena Bay Yacht Club) in 2011 and became quite active in our group. They are Lu Abel and his wife Diane Nelson Abel. Diane volunteered to develop and write a brochure to market our yacht club and asked me to provide some photographs for it. As I corresponded with Diane I noticed her signature box says that she is a book coach/editor/publisher. She agreed to help me complete my goal of telling my story of surviving the worst aviation disaster in world history and has been instrumental in structuring, developing and editing this book. My sister Marcia believes that this arrangement was indeed Divine Intervention. Let the story be told.

I discovered the yacht club has other talented members. In addition to my editor, I also met my graphic designer, Gwyn Smith there. I thank them both for their collaboration and for helping me bring my survival story to life.

I also want to thank my Ukiah High School senior class English teacher, Norm Williamson, for his excellent teaching skills. He taught us to "write with examples." Make a statement of three to five sentences and then write three example paragraphs that support that statement. His instructions are still with me after all these years (since 1966). I have written articles for newsletters, including The Whale's Tale for Ballena Bay Yacht Club, but this book is by far the biggest writing task I have undertaken.

Another one of my friends from the club is a retired 747 pilot with United Airlines, Willie Winquist. He told me several times that I should write a book about my experience surrounding the Canary Islands aircraft accident. During his last several years with United, Willie was a Line-check Airman. In that capacity he flew with experienced pilots and observed their actions and capabilities in the cockpit. United Airlines was the first airline to embrace the concept of Crew Resource Management.

Willie has been a champion of my endeavor to write my story. He and his wife Karen live in Denver, Colorado and are partners in a 36 foot sailboat, SWEET SACRIFICE, with his brother Wayne. Wayne lives nearby in Mountain View and is on the boat quite often. He is actually more active in the yacht club now as he serves on the board of directors. Willie and Karen are on their boat several times a year and were in the club for our annual crab feed in January. We discussed the progress of my writing project and I provided an update. As I left the clubhouse to walk back to my boat I had an idea. I turned around and went back to the club and spoke with Willie again. I asked him if he would be willing to write a piece for my book. He responded that he would be honored to write something for me. Thank you very much for your contribution Willie!

I want to thank Dick Folger of Folger Graphics in Hayward, California, and his team, for the great results of reproducing some of my photographs for this book. The cover photograph of the burning Pan Am 747 shows some details that I never knew existed. His technician, Mathew Revak, did a great job of bringing out those details. This photo and others like it were published in the Dutch magazine, *Niewe Review*, without my permission or compensation. My book provides details about how that happened.

After I starting this writing project I developed the idea of contacting our co-pilot that day in Tenerife, First Officer Bob Bragg. I tried a couple of ideas online but got no results. Then I looked up Pan Am and found a website devoted to former employees. I sent them a message detailing that I am a survivor of the Tenerife accident and am writing a book about my experience. I asked them to forward my message to Bob Bragg. The next day I received a message from Bob that read: This is Bob. Call me. I called the following day and there he was! I was so excited! I recognized his voice and we spoke for a while about my book. He was very supportive of my effort in that we both want to make the details of this accident well known so that it never happens again.

FOREWORD

On March 27, 1977, when I was 29 years old, I survived the world's most deadly aircraft accident at Tenerife in the Canary Islands. This accident involved two fully loaded 747s that were on the ground in fog and collided when KLM initiated a takeoff roll while Pan Am was still on the runway. Almost 600 people died. I am one of the initial 74 survivors and one of only fourteen walking survivors.

It was not easy for me to write about this near-death experience. That date has become my second birthday and jumps out at me whenever I see it in print. I think most people feel that way when they see their birth date mentioned in any media. I still have the feeling that this accident was not real and could not have happened. But I know that the event was real because I still have some pain in my lower back and a small lump on the side of my head.

The other big reminders of that day are the photographs I took that afternoon. I was one of two photographers that day and include copies of some of my photos in this book. My undeveloped film was stolen from me by a Dutch journalist named Hans Hofman and subsequently published in Europe without my permission or any compensation.

At the time of the accident I was David Wiley, and that name appears on the list of survivors of the Canary Islands aircraft accident. I had a falling out with my father in 1987 and was so mad that I hired an attorney and filed a petition with a local court to change my name. In 1987 I became David Yeager Alexander. Floyd Alexander was my mother's stepfather and the only grandfather that I knew on her side of the family.

Here is my personal story of survival and renewal, with a second chance at life. It is an eyewitness account of what it was like to be inside one of the largest aircraft in the world when everything went terribly wrong and when the rules in aviation were not followed correctly. I detail how I recovered from that tragedy and went flying again, traveling all over the world.

I also include the English translation of the final report about the accident by the Department of Aviation and Commerce of the Government of Spain. Many passengers do not know what is going on in the cockpit of the aircraft on which they are a passenger. Flying today is a carefully choreographed dance, or movement, both on the ground and in the air. Most pilots expect what to hear from both the ground controller and the air controller. If any unusual words are spoken they immediately know that something is wrong.

Ever since the accident, I am frequently asked what happened—how did it happen—how did I survive—how have I fared since—and could it ever happen again? I was so traumatized by the accident that I couldn't bring myself to revisit it in my mind or to write about it for 35 years. Now I am ready to tell my story.

AFTERWORD: THE TENERIFE CRASH FROM AN AVIATOR'S PERSPECTIVE

On a fog-covered runway in 1977, two aircraft collided in the largest aviation disasters in history. Over thirty five years later, what have we learned? How did the worst disaster in aviation history change the future of aviation safety?

William G. Winquist, Captain, Retired, United Airlines

Pilots encounter an average of three threats on a typical flight. And, on a typical flight, pilots average two pilot errors of varying significance. On March 27, 1977 a series of threats, pilot errors, and unique circumstances killed some 583 people when two Boeing 747 jumbo jets collided on a fog-covered runway at Los Rodeos Airport, on the Spanish island of Tenerife.

Both flights were charter flights—one Pan Am (American) and one KLM (Dutch) aircraft. Both flights were destined for the Spanish island of Palmas de Gran Canaria, Spain. And both flights diverted to Tenerife.

The Pan Am 747-121 was a charter from Los Angeles to Palmas de Gran Canaria, carrying 396 people including 16 crew members. The jet had been in the air for eight hours when it was diverted to Tenerife because a bomb exploded in Palmas de Gran Canaria two hours earlier, and the airport was closed for repairs. The Pan Am jet made an uneventful approach and landing at Tenerife only to find a large number of aircraft at the airport, including a KLM 747-206B charter flight with 248 people including 14 crew. Like the Pan Am aircraft, the KLM had been diverted to Tenerife.

The small Tenerife airport, 70 kilometers from Palmas de Gran Canaria, was overwhelmed with diversions from the neighboring island and both crews and passengers were unhappy about the delay. The Pan Am jet was parked on the tarmac behind the KLM aircraft. The KLM captain was reported to be stressed about the delay. Because Dutch regulations forbade the KLM crew from exceeding their limit flight hours, the crew and the company would be in serious trouble if the KLM could not take off soon.

After hours of waiting, air traffic control finally directed the Pan Am aircraft to taxi down the fog-covered runway behind the KLM aircraft. At the time, the runway center line lighting was reportedly not functioning. The Pan Am aircraft was directed to taxi off the runway at the third taxiway on the left, while the KLM aircraft was directed to continue taxiing to the takeoff end and make a U-turn-and-hold position. This should have allowed the KLM aircraft to take off with the

Pan Am jet safely off to the side of the runway. But the Pan Am crew inadvertently passed the third taxiway in the heavy fog.

As the air traffic controller was beginning to give the KLM crew its air traffic control clearance, the Pan Am jet was approaching the fourth taxiway and beginning to exit—but one taxiway late. In the fog, the air traffic controller could not see the Pan Am jet, and ordered the KLM to position and hold. Although air traffic control was supposed to give the all-clear for the runway before the KLM jet began its takeoff procedures, the KLM captain either did not understand or did not hear the hold order from air traffic control. Despite the hold order and the copilot questioning the position of the Pan Am jet, the KLM captain initiated takeoff with the Pan Am jet still on the runway. By the time the KLM captain could see the Pan Am jet exiting the runway, it was too late to stop. The KLM crew tried to fly over the Pan Am jet, and the two collided.

The collision and fireball actually cleared the fog for some distance. There were no survivors on the KLM aircraft, and 64 people and the captain and crew survived on the Pan Am aircraft. A total of 583 people died.

Undoubtedly, the accident resulted from a chain of contributing factors, any one of which may have prevented the accident if broken in time.

While we may never know if breaking any particular link in the chain would have prevented the accident, we can learn from this accident and we can implement training procedures to minimize the chances of incidents like this.

The Tenerife disaster was a major impetus for significant changes in pilot training and education. As a leader in flight safety, United Airlines was a major contributor in developing the first crew resource management program called "C/L/R"—standing for Command, Leadership, Resource Management Training. United implemented C/L/R in 1981 and it now includes training for flight attendants, dispatchers and maintenance personnel. The purpose of C/L/R is to maximize flight safety by minimizing the occurrence of airplane accidents and incidents caused by human error. While C/L/R provides a means of assessing personal work habits and interpersonal relationships, it is also a valuable tool when used in the threat and error environment. In achieving flight safety, C/L/R promotes vigilance over complacency. C/L/R has become the standard for crew training. The latest designators for these programs are (CRM) Crew Resource Management, and (TEM) Threat and Error Management.

As a retired 747-400 Captain, Line-check Airman, and Flight Standard Captain, I have had the benefit of not only having this training as part of my own aviation education, but of teaching the principles to others. Managing crew resources in the cockpit requires soliciting input and listening when critical statements are made. For example, had the KLM captain listened and reacted when his copilot said "Is he not clear, the Pan American," the takeoff could have been halted for confirmation. Even so, C/L/R and the newer variations of it are not a magic bullet. There are inherent threats and opportunities for errors in aviation. Above all, pilots must recognize their limits and realize that they can make mistakes. Without this constant awareness, the benefits of even the best training program can be lost. Pilots must focus on the threats and errors they observe and be proficient in both threat and error countermeasures. These are vital parts of threat and error awareness and are necessary to achieve the highest level of safety. Programs like C/L/R, CRM and TEM are not stand-alone activities; they must be integrated into all aspects of the aviation profession.

Crew Resource Management and Threat and Error Management are one of the most beneficial results of the constantly advancing educational and training tools in aviation.

David Alexander, a survivor of Tenerife and a good friend, wrote this account of one of the worst disasters in aviation history. I am hopeful it will be read by commercial pilots and airline personnel around the world.

Thank you, David.

PART ONE

How the world's deadliest plane crash changed my life.

～ Chapter 1 ～

MY LIFE BEFORE THE ACCIDENT

My father was a minister so we moved frequently and lived in a number of states. Everywhere that we lived, I was bullied and tormented by neighborhood kids because I have had a speech defect since birth. I compensated by developing a hobby of photography at an early age and by concentrating on my fascination with world geography and with boats.

Ironically, I think both learning to deal with bullies and developing these passions helped me through the aftermath of the world's deadliest plane crash and fueled my refusal to spend the rest of my life living in fear.

My father was an avid photographer so maybe I got the idea from him by watching him document what was going on around us.

When I was 11 years old we lived in the small town of Broken Bow, Nebraska. One day I found a camera outside. I used some of my allowance money to buy black and white film and get my photos developed. I photographed the parsonage where we lived, next to the First Christian Church, where my father was the minister. The first taste of disaster came not long after that when Brown's Furniture Store, just across the street, caught on fire and burned to the ground. I quickly got my camera and documented what I saw that day. I still have those pictures and will treasure them forever.

Ever since I was a little boy I have also been fascinated with boats. As a second grader in Bremerton, Washington, on Puget Sound, I took a big drawer out of an old dresser stored in the garage and carried it down to the water to find out if it would float. My mother and I walked to the nearby shore to test out my idea. Mom was willing to let me try to make a boat out of this dresser drawer. I wanted to get in it and paddle out from shore to see what it was like. Even though the drawer sank right away, I was still enchanted with that idea. We took the drawer back home and put it back in its place in the garage.

A little while later we moved to Twin Falls, Idaho, in south central Idaho.

Twin Falls is near the Snake River and was home to Shoshone Falls and Twin Falls. Both of these waterfalls had good sized bodies of water behind them used for recreational boating. When I was there with my family I liked to walk out on the docks to watch boats leave and return. I made myself useful by catching a dock line as a boat arrived and securing it to a cleat mounted to the dock. I was not allowed to go with anyone in their boat but I had so much fun just watching the boats on the water.

Throughout most of my childhood, I was a victim of bullying. I was a special needs student during first and second grade because I had difficulty speaking. The special education school provided me with a speech therapist, which was very helpful. My family moved to Twin Falls, Idaho, as I entered third grade and it was determined that I was ready for "mainstream" public school. The transition was OK for me. I made friends in church and I made friends in my class at school.

I had one close friend in the neighborhood whose family lived across the street from us. He was about my age, as I recall, and we enjoyed playing together. A group of neighborhood boys made life miserable for me, however. Going to and from school, while walking or riding my bike, was a challenge. The neighborhood bullies, led by Jerry Jones, attacked me in the winter with snowballs and rocks or sticks in other seasons. I tried to fight back but I was uncoordinated and could not defend myself very well. I usually tried to avoid them.

One day, while walking home from school Jerry Jones rode right past me on his bike but did not attempt to harass me. That's when I realized that he, like most bullies, would not attack when they were alone. When there was a group together they fed off each other and then attacked. Jerry was being raised in a single parent home by his mother. His older brother was in state prison at that time. I don't know what crime he was serving time for but Jerry did not seem to get the message. I have wondered from time to time whatever happened to him as he grew into his twenties. How many other victims are there?

Children can be cruel. One time at the Twin Falls church some of the boys pushed me into the ladies bathroom, then held the door shut so that I could not escape that embarrassment. I complained to my dad later in the week and his response was to try not to "rock the boat." He encouraged me to get along with other kids and understand that they were just playing. He did not want to cause a problem with his Board members as they held his job in their hands. This time-frame was the first time I heard my dad comment in the pulpit that if MY kids are misbehaving, it was because they were hanging out with the elders' and deacons' kids! The assaults continued for the next three years in Idaho.

I was glad when I was told that we were going to move again. When I was in the fifth grade in January 1959, we moved to Broken Bow, Nebraska, a town in the middle of the state on Highway 2. I made a great friend there named Tom Cunningham whose family belonged to our church, where my father, Ralph, was the minister. Tom lived just outside of town on a small farm and invited me to join him there on many Sunday afternoons. There was always something to do outdoors, like playing with the hand-cranked tractor or walking along a creek.

In Broken Bow there were times when I was attacked while going to or from school just as before. I got better at dodging the bad kids. My paternal grandmother, Edith, bought me a bicycle. One afternoon as I was riding home from school, probably junior high by then, I was attacked by a fellow student walking on the sidewalk. He picked up a piece of dried branch and threw it at me. I still remember seeing it spiraling towards me like a Frisbee. I saw it coming and ducked down lower on my bike. That maneuver did not work and I was hit in the head. I almost crashed my bike but held on to outrun the attacker. His father was the Broken Bow superintendent of schools so I got some sympathy from my parents but little else.

In August, 1962, we moved, again, from Nebraska to Ukiah, California, a two hour drive north of San Francisco. I was glad to leave the hot, humid summer and very cold, snowy winters for the mild weather near the Pacific coast.

That fall I started my freshman year of high school. I discovered that bullies did not take difficult classes so I got away from them by taking college prep courses and electronics courses where I was surrounded by other students who were intent upon getting an education. Both of my parents were college graduates and I realized by then that an education beyond high school was essential to a successful life as an adult. The physical assaults became less frequent over time though I occasionally confronted deadbeat bullies while walking to and from school.

In my sophomore year at Ukiah High I took an electronics class and found that I loved it. I took the second year of that program as a junior as well. We learned to build a simple AM radio, back in the day of vacuum tubes before transistors. Imagine a thin board like Masonite (their plant was in Ukiah) with small holes in it arranged in straight lines. Into the holes at certain places we would place springs that stood straight up. The various radio components were connected together by the springs. First we studied a schematic, or drawing, of the radio, and then placed the components on the board in the correct sequence. The last component was the speaker. I was the first student in the class to get my radio to work and was so excited! We had studied different types of circuits, including power supplies and oscillators (which create signals at a specific frequency). But now we put them together and made something that worked as a system. I was SO impressed and amazed! This was really cool. It was then that I realized that I wanted to work in this field.

At first I wanted to be an engineer and develop new products. Soon I decided I would rather be a technician because I wanted to work directly with products, hands on. Plus, the study of math was not as intense. Our teacher, Mr. Coonrod, who also taught woodworking which I took during my freshman year at Ukiah, was very good at explaining the theory of how each component worked and how they worked together as a system or circuit. That was the beginning of a career for me in the high tech field.

My senior year was my best year of high school. I had earned the respect of most of my classmates because I persevered through the daunting challenge of upper level class work and physical harassment.

I had one more unpleasant surprise during my senior year. I was assaulted in a hallway and my glasses were knocked off. One of the lenses broke which left me with a vision problem for several weeks until the new lens was ready. The attacker was identified right away and pulled out of class. My father was called and he came to the principal's office. After a short discussion it was agreed that the attacker would pay for a new lens for me. I got a lot of sympathy from my classmates and teachers. I was temporarily moved to the front of the classroom to be closer to the blackboard so that I could see it better. After about four weeks the new lens arrived and I could see well again.

The student who knocked my glasses off was unhappy with the resulting punishment. His father owned a dry cleaning store in Ukiah and after school the student drove the company van around town, making home deliveries. One afternoon as I was walking home from school he drove past me. He stopped the van, got out and walked towards me with his fists clenched. I had no doubt about his intentions. I circled around the van so he could not catch me. When another car drove by, he gave up on the attack, returned to the van and drove off. I told my parents about it but nothing ever happened. Since there were no witnesses, there was no case. Plus my dad was still adamant about not rocking the boat by fighting back. His attitude changed much later in life but it was too late for me.

I graduated from Ukiah High School in June of 1966 with the largest class in the school's history. Four hundred sixty-five of us walked across the platform to get our diplomas! Most of the high school bullies did not make it that far. One of them died in a car crash that summer after graduation and another one went to jail.

For most of my adult life I felt that I was picked on as a child because I was "different." Most bullies probably felt that I was an easy target who could or would not fight back. Recently though, in my early retirement years, I have found that other people with no perceived weakness were also attacked by bullies. Bullies, in general, build themselves up by tearing other people down. Some bullies attack animals instead of people, or in addition to people. It's not MY fault that I was a target. Bullies just look for a vulnerable victim to attack.

Floyd Alexander my mother's stepfather and my only grandfather on her side of the family gave me some money when I was a student at Santa Rosa Junior College, in Santa Rosa, California, so that I could finish the second and final year of the Electronic Technology program. It was a robust basic electronics background and included the fairly new technology of microwave technology. That education served me well throughout my career until one tech job was relocated to Malaysia and the next one to Thailand.

My first job was with Teledyne MEC in Palo Alto which manufactured microwave amplifiers, called traveling wave tubes. Most employers were looking for applicants with basic knowledge of the field to which they would add their own specialized training. The basic circuits, like amplifiers and oscillators, are used in that frequency range but they look different than in lower digital frequency ranges. After my job interview with a tour of the production line, during which I explained to the supervisor/interviewer how their amplifier system worked with the measurement of power input and power output, I was offered a job on the spot. The excitement I felt was tremendous! Two years of hard work paid off. I reported for work the following Monday, September 30, 1968.

Nearly all of Teledyne MEC's products had military applications. My job was to tune and test a low power microwave amplifier model which was part of an airborne anti-missile system built by Westinghouse and designed to detect the incoming radar signals from a guided missile and guide it away from the aircraft. It was housed in a pod mounted under the wing of the F4 Phantom jet fighter, the hottest thing in the sky at the time. I couldn't serve in the military but I felt that I served in another way which helped to keep our pilots safe, especially over North Vietnam.

Other than my work which I loved, my adult life before the accident in Tenerife was rather boring. I did not want to stay home so I went out to the movies a lot, sometimes on Saturday afternoon and again that night and repeated with two more movies on Sunday. I went by myself as I was not dating anyone during this time. I got involved in computer dating through an agency and had a few dates but I didn't meet anybody who interested me.

I also liked to go for drives on the weekend afternoons. Palo Alto is an hour's drive away from the Pacific Ocean. I liked to visit Santa Cruz and its amusement park facing the beach. My favorite ride was the roller coaster The Big Dipper, an old fashioned wood model. The first rise was a BIG one followed by an equally big drop and turn! One day I rode it three times.

There is a long pier nearby where I liked to see commercial fishing boats and wildlife. Seals and sea lions in the water below the walkway barked to get attention from the patrons above. We could buy small bags of raw fish to feed the barking seals. I liked being near the water and enjoyed my time there.

Another favorite place was on San Francisco Bay. Palo Alto hosted a small marina near the municipal airport and the golf course. When I was not looking at the boats, I was watching the small general aviation airplanes taking off and landing at the airport. After much thought about it I decided against pursuing my interest in aviation by learning how to fly. I decided that I did not have the nerves for it plus there was not as much social interaction at the airport as there was in a marina.

I also hung out at Redwood City's two large and one small San Francisco Bay marinas. Pete's Harbor had a public access sales dock adjacent to the fuel dock. I met some people with a small power boat for sale but I did not have the money to buy it outright. I was unwilling to go into debt to satisfy my interest in boating but I contined to hang out there and eat at the Harbor House Restaurant which overlooked the marina and the channel that led out to the bay. From then on, my dream was to own a boat and explore San Francisco Bay.

My third life passion has always been music. I grew up in a musical family and I was the oldest child. My mother Lois played both the organ and piano for church services. My father Ralph played the clarinet in high school in Nampa, Idaho. My sister Marcia also played the clarinet at Ukiah High school. My brother Dan played several instruments in the same high school band, including the clarinet and tuba. At one point he also became the band major, leading the band in parades. My younger sister Cheryl had no interest in music.

In the mid-1970s, I bought my first of two organs from a store in a small Mountain View mall. The owner was a pretty sharp business person. The store's front room held about 25 organs, set in rows, facing the main aisle of the mall. If you bought an organ from them, you could come in at various times during the week and participate in group lessons. Also, with the purchase came five free private lessons with a teacher. I had moved from a very small first instrument to a spinet console made by Conn. I wasn't all that skilled but I enjoyed playing. The store hosted a free concert almost every Sunday afternoon at 2 pm which drew 25 or 30 people who listened to a sales person or a guest artist play and demonstrate the big three-manual (keyboard) console. That inspired the rest of us to practice so that we could play like them.

Jerry, my next door neighbor in the Creekside Trailer Lodge mobile home park where I lived at the time, also played an organ that he bought from the same dealer. He liked the Yamaha whereas I liked the sound and tone of the Conn organ. We liked to listen to each other play and share ideas for new music.

Playing music is an emotional experience. Sometimes musicians are happy with the piece they are playing or they may be sad. The song has a connotation or history with it and playing it brings out those emotions.

∽   Chapter 2   ≍

ON THE WAY TO THE GOLDEN ODYSSEY

In the spring of 1977 I made plans to go on my second cruise. The previous summer I went on a one-week Caribbean cruise and really enjoyed the days at sea. That cruise with Norwegian Caribbean Lines stopped in Haiti, Puerto Rico, St. Thomas and Dominican Republic.

I liked that first cruise so much that I decided to take a two-week cruise through the Mediterranean Sea. I wanted to see many different civilizations so I chose one with Royal Cruise Lines that started in Las Palmas, Canary Islands (which are off the northwest coast of Africa opposite Morocco) and ended in Athens, Greece. The Greek-owned ship was the Golden Odyssey, which was relatively small at 10,500 tons and launched just three years earlier. She carried 120 crew members to look after 500 passengers.

Intermediate ports of call were: Funchal, Madeira, Casablanca, Morocco with a side trip to the capital of Rabat, Tangier, Morocco, then across the entrance to the Mediterranean Sea to Gibraltar, Palma, Mallorca, Tunis, Tunisia, Valletta, Malta, Heraklion, Crete, a pass through Santorini, an extinct volcano, and finally, Athens, Greece.

Pan Am Flight 1477 was a charter flight originating in Los Angeles, California (LAX) with an intermediate stop in New York (JFK) where we added more passengers, changed the flight and service crews, and serviced the aircraft. That particular 747 named Clipper Victor was set up for charter service and had more seats than usual. The seats were assigned by Royal Cruise Line of San Francisco and my assigned seat was 30C, an aisle seat on the left aisle, the row in front of the exit door over the wing.

Living in Palo Alto, California, at that time, I flew south to Los Angeles (LAX) from San Francisco (SFO) and arrived at the gate of the international terminal around noon on Saturday, March 26, 1977. Lots of people were there, waiting for

19

our plane to arrive. The gate agent announced that the plane was returning from South America and would be two hours late. That turned out to be a factor that put us in mortal danger. I noticed that most of the passengers were in their 60s. I was 29 at the time and looked forward to making new friends and seeing new places.

A woman was walking around the gate area visiting with the passengers and introducing them to a friend of hers. The lady was Enid Tartikoff, a Royal Cruise Lines employee and the person she was introducing was the chef from our cruise ship, Golden Odyssey. The chef was a short guy with a mustache and he was smoking. (It's hard to believe now that people were allowed to smoke in the terminal and on airplanes in those days.) We met and shook hands and I watched them make their way through the crowd. The cruise line had flown the chef out to the west coast of the United States to learn more about California cuisine.

Our plane that was to carry us to Las Palmas in the Canary Islands finally arrived about two hours late. I got out my camera and took a picture of it as it stood at the gate. I had been on a Western Airlines ("The only way to fly!" was the tagline in their TV commercials) McDonnell-Douglas DC-10 to Hawaii in 1973 but this was my first flight on a Boeing 747. I think all of us were excited to get on the plane and be on our way.

This was no ordinary flight. We were on our way to board the Golden Odyssey, and see interesting sights in the Mediterranean Ocean. We finally started boarding and I made my way down the left aisle of this huge airplane to my assigned seat, 30C. I was carrying my camera bag with me and set that under the seat in front of me. Inside the bag were my travel documents, including plane tickets and ship boarding pass. I also had my passport in there. (That turned out to be a mistake I never made again. After this trip I always carried it in my shirt pocket.)

As I settled into my seat I introduced myself to my seatmates, a married couple probably in their 50s, a little younger than most of the passengers. I don't remember their names, which is quite unfortunate, as they were very kind to me. The husband sat next to me and his wife by the window. Back to back behind us were jump seats for three flight attendants by the exit door over the left wing.

Finally, the door closed and we were ready to depart. A tug pushed our giant plane back from the gate and we made our way out to our assigned runway for takeoff. We were all pleased to be on our way even if we were two hours behind schedule.

Our flight stopped in New York to pick up about 23 more passengers. There was a change of flight and service crew. In a quick turnaround of about an hour, the plane was serviced with food for the passengers and fuel for the plane. We passengers stayed on the plane. Then we were on our way again, departing around 11 pm, local time.

The flight to Las Palmas, Canary Islands, was about eleven hours. We watched the sun come up and saw lots and lots of water. Most of the passengers tried to sleep as it was our bedtime. I don't sleep well on a plane but managed to catnap several times. I think it was during this leg of the flight that the couple across the aisle from me spoke with a couple sitting several rows forward of us and arranged to change seats. Those seats in the center section backed up to the toilets so the seat backs did not recline very far, if at all. The man who was originally assigned that seat was very tall so the seat was even more uncomfortable for him. The new passengers across the aisle from me in seats 30D and E were Col. Albert and Florence Trumbull of San Diego. They were in their early 70s and were on their honeymoon. During the flight, the couple they changed seats with stopped by to say thank you for helping them. Albert and Florence were pleased to help them out. It was a fateful change.

The sun was fully up and we passengers were starting to rouse from fitful slumber. The flight attendants started breakfast service. We were about two and a half hours from our destination of Las Palmas and still over the broad Atlantic Ocean. After our breakfast trays were picked up by our flight attendants, we were more alert and looking out the windows.

About an hour before landing, our captain, Victor Grubbs, came on the PA system and announced a change of plans. He told us that a bomb had exploded aboard a jetliner on the ground at the airport in Las Palmas. That airport was closed and all inbound traffic was to divert to Tenerife. That was the end of his announcement. I noticed an immediate turn of the plane to the left. We passengers then began to question the flight attendants about the location of Tenerife. Most of the passengers, including myself, had never heard of Tenerife. They patiently explained to us that Tenerife was a neighboring island in the Canary Islands chain and was just a short distance away from the main island of Grand Canary and its airport of Las Palmas. We were concerned about getting to the ship on time as we were already two hours late leaving Los Angeles. The Golden Odyssey's departure time was that afternoon and we were anxious to get there.

Looking out my window I got my first glimpse of Tenerife. I saw a lush green mountain with a narrow green valley below it open on one end to the ocean. The airport seemed to be in the middle of that valley. We came in rather high over the airport, then turned right and made a long loop and came back to the final approach track. We were still high and made another loop. As we turned away the second time, some of the passengers became worried and wondered what the problem was. On our third approach, we came in lower and then the nose dropped and I told my seatmates that we were going to land this time. Sure enough we "jumped the fence" at the outer border of Los Rodeos Airport on the island of Tenerife.

After a smooth landing we taxied left off the main runway, taxied to an open spot on the tarmac and stopped. Soon we could tell that the left front door opened and stayed open. We sat there for about two hours while the captain informed us what was happening around us and at Las Palmas. Captain Grubbs announced that we were allowed to walk out the left front door onto the top of the stairs but we were not allowed to go down the stairs, because that would cause a problem with the immigration officials.

Since I had never been to Tenerife or the Canary Islands, I decided to walk out on the stairway and take some pictures. I pulled my camera bag out from under the seat in front of me, hung my 35mm SLR camera around my neck and proceeded up the left aisle to the open door. As I got out on the stairway platform I noticed another 747 parked in front of us. Several other aircraft were between us. The 747 had a KLM insignia on it and was turned slightly to the left. I took a photo looking straight ahead of us taking in all of the planes parked there. Then I turned to my left and took two more photos of the open green fields surrounding the airport. I didn't notice the mountain that I saw from the air as that was on the other side of the plane. I was in no big hurry to get back to my seat so I just stood there for a while and took in all the scenery. I think there were more airplanes on the ground behind us as well.

As I took in the sights around the airport, I heard the captain's voice again. Captain Grubbs had previously announced that because of the delay in Tenerife, he was opening the bar for free drinks. I do not drink alcohol so I didn't care too much about that. Soft drinks were free anyway. Then he announced that he was opening the cockpit to visitors. Anyone could walk up to the upper deck and see what the cockpit looked like. Well, I was all for that! I love airplanes (and still do) and I wanted to check it out. Plus I could see the upper first class seating area.

I climbed the spiral staircase that led to the upper first class seating area and the cockpit. At the top of the stairs was our co-pilot, Bob Bragg who welcomed us to the cockpit area. As I stepped to the cockpit doorway, I saw Flight Engineer George Warns sitting at his station, along the right wall of the cockpit. I raised my camera to take a picture and he said just a minute and turned on his control panel lights. Then he slid his seat back to give me a clear view of his part of the cockpit I took another shot of the co-pilot's station, the right seat. Our captain, Victor Grubbs, was in his seat looking straight ahead. He was busy talking or listening to the radio. I tried to hang around a little longer to take it all in but other passengers were coming up the stairway to look around as well. So I headed back to my seat, my lucky seat, 30C.

As I walked back to my seat, a number of people involved in conversation were standing in the aisle and near the exit door. I remember one of the flight attendants assigned to a jump seat right behind me telling people about her horse. She lived in Kentucky or Tennessee. She rode her horse in jumping competitions and was looking forward to riding again. I became rather attached to those three flight attendants. They were trying so hard to take care of us.

I had developed a headache and was not feeling as pleasant as I was earlier.

The lady by the window, in seat 30A, offered me a pill and I felt better. I chatted with the man in front of me in 29C, Norm Williams. I wish that I had paid more attention to him but I was not feeling well. The purser on our flight, the senior flight attendant, had announced earlier that they were about to run out of ice so they were rationing the ice cubes to one per drink. I remember seeing a male passenger walking forward up the left aisle holding on to the back of the seats as he walked along. He was a little drunk and needed the extra stability. I observed that eighty five percent of the passengers on this flight were over 60. I had seen a couple at the gate in LAX with two teenage boys.

PRELUDE TO TRAGEDY

After about three hours on the ground in Tenerife, Captain Grubbs announced that the airport in Las Palmas had reopened and we would be departing soon. A loud cheer and applause rose up from the passengers We were all excited to get on the Golden Odyssey and head out to sea. After another fifteen minutes or so, another announcement said that the captain of the KLM 747 parked in front of us had decided to refuel there instead of at Las Palmas. There was a question as to whether our plane could get by the KLM 747 to get to the main runway. At that point First Officer Bob Bragg and our Flight Engineer George Warns deplaned and paced off the distance between our wingtip and that of the KLM 747. After carefully pacing off the distance, the team found that we were 20 feet short of the clearance needed to get by them and proceed to the active runway. So we had to wait longer while KLM finished the refueling process. After another half hour of waiting, both the KLM and Pan Am 747s were ready to taxi out for takeoff. I don't recall whether or not the flight attendants performed another safety demonstration but I think they did not.

I still had my camera hanging around my neck. I decided to keep it out instead of putting it back in the bag under the seat. There might be some interesting things on the ground in Las Palmas and I was ready to take more pictures. All of a sudden fog began to roll in over us. It moved in very fast and was very thick. I could just barely make out the faint glow of the lights along the runway. I heard the roar of a jet taking off. I couldn't see it but I heard it. It was one of the smaller jetliners on the ground between us and KLM. Then another jet took off in the fog. Just before we started to move, the lady by the window asked me if I would like to change seats so I could take pictures out of the window. I replied, "No. It's foggy now and I can't see anything. I'll just stay here." As we started to move, the passengers gave another round of approving applause. We were all excited to be on our way to our ship.

Captain Grubbs had told us that KLM and Pan Am had been instructed by the tower to proceed down the main runway together with KLM leading the way. Because of the huge crowd of other aircraft on the ground, we could not use the taxiways to get to the far end of the main runway. The captain said that when KLM got to the end of the runway, they would turn around and hold that position. We would take the last exit and move in behind them. Then they would take off, then we would take off. It would be just a short 15-minute flight to Las Palmas. This did not seem like a normal maneuver to me. It sounded simple enough but the fog added more of a challenge to the process. I was rather apprehensive and I found out later that other passengers felt the same way. Some of them asked to be allowed off the plane but the captain refused their request.

⤳ Chapter 4 ⤶

IMPACT!

I was quite nervous about the lack of visibility because of the thick, obscuring fog. It had moved in very fast. Partway along our slow taxi to the far end of the main runway I noticed that we began a turn to the left. I was looking out the window past my seatmates when something caught my eye. As I looked forward, I saw smoke rolling in from the first class cabin. Then, instantaneously, the plane came to a hard stop! It was so hard that I was thrown forward in my seat and I leaned over. Something hit me on the head, knocked my glasses off, and was lying on top of me.

Out of the corner of my left eye I could see the couple next to me move away from me, then down. I raised my right arm and with all my might, I threw off whatever it was that was on top of me. As I leaned back in my seat, I was looking upwards and I saw blue sky! There was a hole in the ceiling about four feet wide and twenty feet long. Small flames flickered around this opening and the smoke was very thick. The smoke burned all the way down my throat into my lungs. My first thought was "I am going to die." Then I said to myself "No I'm not!" I did not even reach down to get my glasses. With one swift move I unbuckled my seatbelt and stood up.

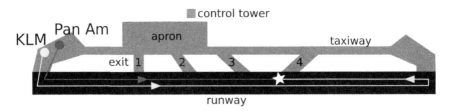

Simplified map of Tenerife runway, taxiways, and aircraft. The star indicates the location of impact.

There are several blank spots in my memory of the next few seconds but it seemed that I turned around to my right, climbed up on my seat, then on to the back of my seat, then out a small hole. I may have moved some wires out of the way. As my memory comes back, I walk down a slight slope and I'm out on the left wing. I look forward to my right and I see that the entire front of the plane is enveloped in smoke. I can't even see it. The inboard engine is on fire with flames rising on both sides of the cowling. Then I see the woman on the wing.

A woman is lying on the wing on her back with her head towards me. She has grey hair and is wearing a dark blue pantsuit. Her arms are raised towards me. I see her lips moving. I cannot hear her but I know that she is saying to me "Help me! Help me!" She is sliding forward, towards the inboard engine fire. Because the nose wheel of our 747 was off the runway and in the grass, the leading edge of the wing was lower than the trailing edge. That's why she was sliding forward. I rushed over to her and grabbed her wrists. Then my memory goes blank again. It seems that I pulled her away from the fire, then out on the wing to a point between the two engines.

When my memory comes back again, I am standing on the leading edge of the wing between the engines. I look down and see green. It's grass. I held my camera in my right hand so that it wouldn't fly up and hit me in the face. I step off the wing and fall feet first to the ground. As I landed, I used a technique I learned in judo class when I was a student at Santa Rosa Junior College. I rolled forward into the gravel and landed on my hands. When I hit the ground, my hearing came back. I did not hear anything inside the plane after impact except a murmur of voices that said "OOOOoooo."

On the ground I heard this loud booming voice in front of me. I recognized the voice as that of our first officer, Co-pilot Bob Bragg. He was screaming, "Run! Run!" I got up and I ran! I ran through the tall wet grass that grew between the two runways. When I got to the parallel runway I stopped and looked back.

Surprisingly, the fog had completely lifted by then. The plane was not burning too badly then. I saw lots of smoke and flames here and there. I looked down the runway. Looking to my right I saw KLM about 400 yards down the runway. It was sitting crossways on the runway with the right side towards me. Its nose wheel was folded back and the fuselage was cracked open crossways behind the dome. Because of that damage, the nose was touching the ground. The tail section was broken in a similar way, cracked open crossways with the tail touching the ground. A huge fire was centered around the main landing gear, which was in its normal down and locked position. Flames were shooting down to the ground then up as high as the top of the fuselage. The flames were just enormous! There was a resulting huge plume of smoke. I saw no one moving there.

At about 40 to 60 seconds after impact I saw a gas explosion from near the left wingtip of the Pan Am plane. The fireball shot straight up into the air about 80 feet and burned for just a few seconds. As it started to subside and come down, the wind caught it and blew flames towards the fuselage. Then the entire plane caught on fire. I ran farther away, across the parallel runway and stopped again.

Because of my training as a microwave technician, working on amplifiers, I understood the need for documentation. What happened and what did it look like? I held up my camera and took the first shot. Then I checked the internal light meter, found that it was too dark, adjusted the F stop and took four more pictures of the burning wreckage. Then I noticed blood on the right side of my head. At first I thought my right ear had been cut off. I didn't care. I was just happy to be alive. But it was still there, so, gently, I pulled on it. It was still attached so I reached into my right rear jeans pocket and pulled out my hand-kerchief. I wiped the blood off my head and realized that I wasn't hurt too bad. I vaguely remember somebody walking by me, pointing a camera at me. Then I sat down on the ground and began to cry.

⤳ Chapter 5 ⤶

SHOCK! AND REALIZATION

Farm workers in the fields next to the airport came over the fence and out to the runway. The first ambulance drove up and I waved it off. The second one arrived moments later and the men opened the back door and put me inside. The doors closed and off we went. A man lying on his back on the floor had a bad cut across the bridge of his nose. So I retrieved my handkerchief and put it on the wound. Another injured man was sitting opposite me on the bench seat. I don't remember his condition but he was sitting upright on his own. That was pretty good.

We were on the highway soon, racing along, then slowed down. A police officer waved us away from the building there and off we went again, in the same direction. I was thinking "Here we are out in the middle of nowhere. How are they going to take care of us?" My concerns were unfounded.

We pulled up to a hospital and the staff carried the other men inside. I was taken to a room along a long hallway and sat in a chair. A woman was lying on the examination table in the room. Parts of her clothes were burned off but she was breathing okay. I sat there for a while then asked a nurse where the bathroom or bano was. I made my way down the hallway and realized again how lucky I was.

As I walked back to my assigned examination room seat, I looked in the other rooms along the hallway. I saw a number of burn victims. One man was sitting on an examination table with his hands on the table at his side. The skin on the back of his hand was hanging off by an inch or so. Other people were lying on litters in the hallway. Some of them had remains of burned clothing on them. I was almost back to my room when a nurse led me back to my chair and told me to stay there. I got the impression they were nuns and this was a Catholic hospital. They were providing us with excellent care. The triage process was going well.

After a while the nurse came back into the room and checked out the woman lying on the table. She seemed to be doing fairly well. The nurse left, then quickly returned to me carrying some equipment. She cleaned the wound on the right rear side of my head. Then I saw her pull out a U-shaped needle. She threaded the needle and began to work on me. At first I was a little afraid of the pain. Then I realized that pain was just what I needed. I NEEDED to feel physical pain! The emotional pain I was feeling was overwhelming at times. I felt the needle go in to one side of my scalp, go across the open area and into the skin on the other side of the wound then pulled both pieces of skin together. She repeated the process three times. Then she tied off the thread and left me there. Again, the physical pain felt good.

After a while a man in a white coat pushing a wheelchair came to me and motioned for me to get in. He took me upstairs to the X-ray department. The radiation tech looked at the finished picture of my head then showed it to me. He gave the x-ray to me. He said there was no fracture so I was free to move on to the next stage of the process.

I was wheeled downstairs to a waiting room. I found a chair and sat down. I counted fourteen of us there. All of us had escaped a fiery mess on one of the largest aircraft in the world. We were the fourteen walking survivors that included two flight attendants and twelve passengers

Then I began to hear their stories of survival. A mother with her teenage daughter across the room told us that her husband tossed both of them out of a hole in the plane's side in first class. They looked up from the ground and saw him turn to get another person. There was another explosion in that part of the plane. He died right in front of them. Another man about my age told us he got out of his seat with his roommate following him and headed for an exit. They almost got there when there was a big explosion. He was blown out of the plane but was not too seriously injured. He could not find his roommate.

After a while a nurse came in to the room with a container of syringes. She gave each of us a shot for tetanus. Again, the pain in my hip reminded me that I was alive. It felt good. About ten minutes later the door opened again. Our First Officer Bob Bragg was in a wheelchair and he wanted to check on us. He had a cast on his left foot.

After he chatted with the others for a while, I asked Bob what he saw from the cockpit. He said that he noticed the lights on the KLM 747 were moving toward us in the thick fog. He was coming right at us. Bob took command of the plane from the captain and increased the throttles to the right engines while stepping on the left brake. That moved our plane hard to the left. He thought KLM 747 missed us but as he reached up above the cockpit windows to hit the four big red buttons there he found that they were gone. Those buttons control the fire extinguishers in the engines. As he turned around in his seat he saw that the ceiling of the entire upper first class cabin was gone. Flight Engineer George Warns got his tools out and proceeded to cut the control cable to engine number one. That engine continued to run after impact and would not shut down. The cowling became misaligned and the fan blades were scraping on it, sending a huge shower of sparks out of the front of the engine. He couldn't get it to stop running even after he cut the control cable to the engine.

Then I found out that there were five men in the cockpit at the time of the collision. Joining the three officers were the Pan Am ground crew chief from Las Palmas and an observer. They had flown to Tenerife by helicopter to offer assistance to the cockpit crew. All five crew members in the cockpit had survived.

One of the walking survivors said that about a half hour before we taxied out for takeoff, they noticed that a round piece of carpet at the foot of the stairway leading to the upper deck had begun to rotate. Then a hatch cover opened upwards and two men climbed out of the access hole in the floor. The men then closed the hatch, returned the carpet to its original location and climbed up the stairs. I learned later that this was the Pan Am ground crew chief for Las Palmas. I believe his name is Juan Antonio Munillo Rivas. Recently I learned that the cockpit observer's name is John Cooper. Both men survived but were not listed as survivors on the list but indeed, they are survivors. It's unclear to me how all five of them got out of the burning wreckage. Some of them went over the side to the ground.

One of my co-survivors told me that they looked up from their seats in the lower first class area and noticed that the upper first class seating area was gone, collapsed down to the lower seating area. They saw Co-pilot Bob Bragg standing in the cockpit doorway when part of the floor collapsed and fell into the lower first class cabin. He escaped over the side of the cockpit and jumped to the ground.

A flight attendant told us that she tried to open one of the exit doors and could not open it. As she moved to the other side of the plane, there was another explosion. One of the other flight attendants who had been trying to open that same door was decapitated by the explosion. There were also dead bodies of passengers from the upper first class cabin on the floor of the lower first class cabin. A third explosion blew a hole in the side of the plane and those two flight attendants, Joan Jackson and Suzanne Donovan, were able to escape by jumping to the ground.

After all fourteen of us walking survivors had been treated and released by Candelario Hospital in Santa Cruz we were taken by bus to the Hotel Mencey. By then it was after 8 pm.

An agent from Pan Am stopped by my room on the second floor to gather some information. After my name and home town, he also wrote down my parents' contact information. I wanted them to know that I was alright. He also arranged for some food to be brought to my room as the dining room was closed for the evening. I remember the meal was chicken and rice but I couldn't eat much of it and set the plate outside the room.

Sleep that night was fitful, at best. In the room next to mine were the wife and daughter who had lost their husband and father. They were Pat and Lynda

Daniel from Southern California. I could hear them crying from time to time and thought of how awful it must be for them.

I was very scared as I began to realize how close my own death had been. That night began the almost endless cycle of images and thoughts in my mind. The "what if's" started as well. What if I had changed seats with the woman by the window? What if I couldn't get that debris off of me after impact? But I did NOT change seats and I DID get free of the debris. I am alive! I am ALIVE!

I had a problem with my eyes. Once they were closed, I had a hard time opening them. It was physically painful to open my eyes after sleeping for a while. I thought that this was related to crying so much and stress. (Much later I learned the real cause. I had several cuts across the surface of both eyes.) I also noticed a pain in my lower back. It wasn't too bad but it was noticeable. Probably the sudden stop from the jump off the wing of the burning 747 was the root cause of that discomfort.

The next morning before breakfast I got on the phone to try to call my parents. I was single at the time (and still am) but I wanted to let them know that I was alright. My high school Spanish was not very good and the hotel operator couldn't help me much. I got through an operator in England but she could not put me through to California. So I went to the dining room for some breakfast. Most of the fourteen walking survivors were there. We always sat together for our meals. We had an emotional breakfast, then went back upstairs to our rooms.

One of my fellow survivors was John Amador, who was close to my age. He spoke fluent Spanish and had been employed by the U.S. State Department at the U.S. Embassy in Madrid, Spain. Several of us gathered in the room shared by two of the four surviving flight attendants, Joan Jackson and Suzanne Donovan. Also present were Enid (a Royal Cruise Lines customer services manager) and Jordan Tartikoff. They were the parents of Brandon Tartikoff, who was the chief programmer for the NBC TV network at that time. (At the beginning of our trip, I had met Enid at LAX walking around the gate area and introducing the ship's chef to our group.)

Everyone in the room said that they had spoken with loved ones back home. I mentioned my difficulty in contacting my parents, John asked me to write down their phone number. He made a phone call, hung up, and said the next incoming phone call would be for me. We continued talking for five or six minutes, getting to know each other better. Then the phone rang. This is still very emotional for me even though it happened 35 years ago. I stood up and began to walk to the far side of the room to answer the phone. It was like a horror movie in which my feet were stuck to the floor and I couldn't move. I got to the phone and picked up the receiver. In a very clear voice my mother said "Hello David." "I'm alright," I said and then broke down and began to cry. One of the flight attendants came over to the bed and began to rub my shoulders and reassured me that I was alright. It was just after 11 pm in California and the news was on. A partial list of survivors was posted on the screen and MY name was the first one on the initial list of five names. My name was misspelled but they knew it was me.

My mother, Lois, said that my Teledyne MEC co-worker, Bob Dippel had called them to ask what they had heard about me. All of my co-workers knew that I was going on this trip. Out of 600 employees in the company I knew almost everybody. Bob and another co-worker, Ron Nelson, and I were special friends. We were into photography and enjoyed taking photos. Every three months or so we would get together and have a slide show.

I told my mother that I had suffered a cut on my head that took three stitches and that I had lost my glasses. I had a spare pair at work so I would need these when I returned to Palo Alto. She had been in touch with Pan Am at San Francisco International Airport (SFO) and they were very helpful. Pan Am had just received the early list of survivors as well and relayed that to my parents who still lived in Ukiah. I was SO relieved that they knew that I was alright. I was on cloud nine. After I hung up the phone, I thanked John Amador profusely for helping me contact my parents!

Our moods swung wildly and instantly those first two days after the Sunday afternoon accident. I had survived the worst aviation accident in history. That Sunday afternoon, 544 people died immediately, including everyone on the KLM 747; 74 of us had survived initially. Unfortunately, that number would change over time.

Before lunch on Monday, one day after the accident, the Pan Am representative had arranged for us to visit a local department store to buy clothes or whatever we needed to get back to our homes. We met upstairs in one of the rooms and we were asked to sign a receipt in exchange for $75.00 worth of the local money, Spanish pesetas. Several people wrote on the receipt "Not a release for damages." This was certainly not a trick by the airline to get out of paying damages but some of the more well-traveled survivors wanted to make sure that their rights to damages were not abridged. We boarded a small bus and were taken into the city of Santa Cruz to visit a department store. There was dried blood on the collar of my shirt so I bought a new one. Also, I bought a package of handkerchiefs as I had applied mine to the badly cut nose of a fellow survivor in the ambulance.

Being out in public that day brought out a feeling that was strange to me. I felt like yelling out "Look at me. I am hurting but I am alive. Don't you realize that so many people died?" But of course I didn't do that. The rest of the day was spent at the hotel resting.

During lunch on Monday, the 28th, we endured another traumatic event. Two men of the group of walking survivors had spouses in the hospital so we did not see them very much. The other twelve of us ate meals together at a long table in the dining room at Hotel Mencey. John Amador, who had helped me with the phone call to my parents, sat on one end of the table. I sat next to him and one of the flight attendants sat across from me. Someone at our table said that they heard from another guest at the hotel that two more survivors had been located at a small clinic. At the time, the survivor count was believed to be 72. John saw the other guest in the dining room and went over to speak with him. He came back a few moments later, visibly shaken. The other two survivors were older people and so could not have been his roommate. John broke down and began to cry. Now it was my turn to comfort him. Joan Jackson, one of the two flight attendants in our group of fourteen walking survivors, and I held his hands as he cried for his lost friend and roommate. The reality of this horrendous situation washed over us again.

Various images of the events played over and over in my mind. The fog bank rolls in again, the sudden stop of the plane with the smoke and heat. Dozens and dozens of times a day, I visualized these images.

Tuesday morning after breakfast I was feeling pretty good emotionally, though I was still in shock. I decided to go to Candelario Hospital to see what was going on there. I took a cab there and walked into the main entrance. Down the hall I saw people walking, others were helping others walk as well. Then I saw her! She was one of the other flight attendants. We recognized each other instantly. She had blonde hair. I said "You! Oh my God! I'm so glad to see you!" We embraced and chatted a bit. I remembered that she had been serving on the right side of the aircraft. She had numerous visible bruises but was able to walk okay. She told me that people from the U.S. Air Force were there and they were arranging the medical evacuation of the injured survivors. Then I noticed Air Force personnel in uniform nearby. President Carter had ordered the Air Force to transport the injured and burned survivors to the Brooke Army Hospital Burn Unit in San Antonio, Texas. The flight attendant suggested that I get back to the hotel soon as Pan Am was preparing to fly the walking survivors out as well.

I was feeling pretty good again. I just saw another survivor who was near the part of the plane where I had been sitting. Maybe there were more survivors from that area. It certainly did not seem that way at the time. All of the walking survivors in the hotel were sitting forward, in first class. One woman was sitting in Row 9. At that time my understanding was that there were no survivors between Row 9 and Row 30, which is where I was. And no one behind me got out either. Fortunately, that information was wrong but I didn't learn the details for another three months.

I was only at the hospital for about eight minutes before I took a cab back to the Hotel Mencey. A number of news media people were present in the lobby. I had spoken with a reporter from the *New York Times* as well as a reporter from the *Los Angeles Times* that morning, before I visited the hospital. Both of these men were very professional and respectful of the survivor's dignity. When I returned from the hospital my mood was on an upward swing. We walking survivors suffered unpredictable mood swings, suddenly, with little notice.

Chapter 6

BULLY AND THIEF, HANS HOFMAN STOLE MY PHOTOS

A s I walked into the lobby of Hotel Mencey I was approached by a heavy-set man in his mid-thirties. He said his name was Hans Hofman and he was with the big paper in Amsterdam. He asked me if I would grant him an interview. I was feeling pretty good at that moment so I agreed to speak with him. We walked to an enclosed room with glass walls. When I told him the part of my story about taking pictures of the burning wreckage, he got rather excited. He picked up a nearby phone and spoke in a foreign language, which I assumed to be Dutch. After he hung up the phone he asked me if I would give him my film. I replied that I had friends back home who would like to see my pictures so, no, I would not give him my film.

Hans Hofman was looking for information. He wanted some information that he could sell. Right after the plane crash in Santa Cruz de Tenerife he flew to the island from Amsterdam looking for information to sell to his contacts in the newspaper and magazine business in Holland. He knew that this story would be very important in Holland. Boy, did he get lucky!

Then he asked me if he could make copies of my pictures and I still wasn't sure if I was willing to do that. Then he got adamant and raised his voice slightly and said "Go get your film." Had I not still been in a state of shock, I never would have agreed. But I did.

I got my film and met Hofman in the hotel shop that sold film and other goods. He spoke to the person behind the counter in Spanish. Even though I had two years of Spanish in high school, I did not understand what was being said. However, I noticed that Hans wrote HIS name and room number on the envelope into which the film was placed. I was told that the prints would be ready that afternoon.

I'd get copies of my pictures later that day, he said. I returned to my room for a nap and that Tuesday afternoon was the last time I was in control of my film.

If I had been in a normal state of mind I never would have agreed to have my film developed in the Canary Islands. I planned to develop the slide film when I got home. My friends would like to see the photos for sure. I had no idea that most of the world would like to see them as well. The group of fourteen walking survivors at Hotel Mencey did not realize at the time how far reaching and important this accident would be in the news media. This story was the first item on the local San Francisco Bay Area TV news as well as national news for six weeks! It was the number two story for another four weeks after that. This accident was a very big story, worldwide.

Hans Hofman is a bully who got very lucky that day in Tenerife—I estimate that he earned close to $100,000 USD from the multiple sales he made of my photos.

∂∾ Chapter 7 ∾∂

START OF MY RETURN TRIP HOME

As soon as I was back in my hotel room the phone rang. An operator on the line told me that she had two calls for me. Also, she said, when I finished the first call, I should not hang up as she would then connect me with the second one. I understood her instructions and proceeded with the first call. KNBR Radio of San Francisco was on the line. I told the reporter my story and stated that I had many friends among my co-workers at Teledyne MEC in Palo Alto. I wanted them to know that I was okay. (It just didn't dawn on me that this conversation was recorded on tape and would be played over the air. It made quite an impression at work.) The second call was from my small hometown newspaper, the *Palo Alto Times*. I told the reporter that "I lost everything but me." I added that I thought I would be returning soon as Pan Am was making arrangements for us.

After I got off the phone I felt even better. More people that I cared about would know that I was okay and would be home soon. I just laid down for a nap when the phone rang again

The agent for Pan Am was on the line. He said he had made arrangements to get me to Las Palmas and then head for home, south of San Francisco. We might not get there in time to catch the flight north today but we would for sure in the morning. I agreed to meet him in about half an hour in the lobby of the hotel.

But I had a problem. What about my pictures? I wrote a note to Hans Hofman that included my home address and phone number. I asked him to send the copies and the negatives to me. I went to his room as I had noted the room number he had written on the film envelope. There was no answer when I knocked on the door so I slipped the note under the door. I returned to my room, gathered my things, including my camera, and headed for the lobby.

≈ Chapter 8 ≪

OFFICIAL FINDING OF HOW THE ACCIDENT HAPPENED

The following is a copy of the transcript of the radio traffic on the ground at Los Rodeos Airport, Tenerife, Canary Islands, between KLM flight 4805, Pan Am flight 1736 and the airport tower controllers on March 27, 1977. This report was published in *Aviation Week and Space Technology* on November 20, 1978 and is the official finding of the Accident Commission of the Subsecretary of Civil Aviation in the Spanish Ministry of Transport and Communications. This translation is by the U.S. National Transportation Safety Board. (I did not use all of the report.) Part B contains a transcript of all of the radio traffic AND the cockpit voices as recorded by the CVR, which are coordinated by time with one of the recorders.

Investigation

Flight history: The KLM Boeing 747, registration BH-BUF, took off from Schipol Airport (Amsterdam) at 9:00 hr on March 27, en route to Las Palmas de Gran Craneria. This flight was part of the Charter Series KL 4805/4806 Amsterdam-Las Palmas (Canary Islands)-Amsterdam operated by KLM on behalf of the Holland Travel Group (H.I.N.T.) Rijswilk-Z.H.

The Pan Am Boeing 747 registration N 736 PA, flight number 1736, left Los Angeles International Airport, Calif. U.S.A on March 26,1977 local date, at 0129z (GMT) hours arriving at John F. Kennedy International Airport at 0617z hours. After the plane was refueled and a crew change affected, it took off for Las Palmas de Gran Caneria (Spain) at 0742z.

While the airplanes were in route to Las Palmas, a bomb exploded in the airport passenger terminal. On account of this incident and a warning regarding a possible second bomb, the airport was closed. Therefore, KLM 4805 was diverted to Los Rodeos (Tenerife) Airport, arriving at 1338z on March 27, 1977.

For the same reason, PAA 1736 proceeded to the same airport—its alternate—landing at 1415.

At first the KLM passengers were not allowed to leave the airplane, but after about 20 min. they were all transported to the terminal building by bus. On alighting from the bus, they received cards identifying them as passengers in transit on flight KLM 4805. Later, all the passengers boarded KLM 4805 except the H.I.N.T. company guide, Miss Robina Guiseline Monique Van Lanschot, who remained in Tenerife.

When Las Palmas Airport was opened to traffic once more, the PAA 1736 crew prepared to proceed to Las Palmas, which was the flight's planned destination.

When it attempted to taxi on the taxiway leading to Runway 12, where it had been parked with four other airplanes on account of the congestion caused by the number of flights diverted to Tenerife, they discovered that it was blocked by KLM Boeing 747, Flight 4805, which was located between PAA 1736 and the entrance to the active runway. The first officer and the flight engineer left the airplane and measured the clearance left by the KLM, reaching the conclusion that it was insufficient in order to let PAA 1836 pass by, obliging them to wait until the former has started to taxi.

The PAA 1736 passengers did not leave the airplane during the whole time that it remained in the airport.

KLM 4805 called the tower at 1635 requesting permission to taxi. It was authorized to do so and at 1658 requested to backtrack on Runway 12 for takeoff on Runway 30. "The tower controller first cleared the KLM to taxi to the holding position for Runway 30 by taxiing down the main runway and leaving it by the (third) taxiway to its left." KLM 4805 acknowledged receipt of this message from the tower, stating that it was at that moment taxiing on the runway, which it would leave by the first taxiway in order to proceed to the approach end of Runway 30. The tower controller immediately issued an amended clearance, instructing it to continue to taxi to the end of the runway, where it should proceed to make a backtrack.

The KLM confirmed that it had received the message, that it would make a backtrack, and that it was taxiing down the main runway. The tower signaled its approval, whereupon KLM 4805 immediately asked the tower again if what they should do was to turn left on Taxiway 1. The tower replied in the negative and repeated that it should continue on to the end of the runway and there make a backtrack.

Finally, at 1659, KLM 4805 replied, "OK, sir."

At 1702, the PAA called the tower to request confirmation that it should taxi down the runway.

The tower controller confirmed this, also adding that they should leave the runway by the third taxiway to their left. At 1703.00, in reply to the tower's query to KLM 4805 as to how many runway exits it had passed, the latter confirmed that at the moment they were passing by taxiway C-4. The tower controller told KLM 4805, "OK, at the end of the runway make one eighty and report ready for ATC clearance."

In response to a query from KLM 4805, the tower controller advised both airplanes—KLM 4805 and PAA 1736—that the centerline lights were out of service. The controller also reiterated to PAA that they were to leave the main runway via the third taxiway to their left and that they should report leaving the runway.

At the times indicated, the following conversation took place between the tower and KLM 4805 and PAA 1736 airplanes; with times taken from KLM CVR [cockpit voice recorder]:

1705:44.6 KLM 4805 – The KLM four eight zero five is now ready for takeoff and we are waiting for our ATC clearance (1705:50.77).

1705.53.41 Tower – KLM eight seven zero five you are cleared to the Papa Beacon, climb to and maintain flight level nine zero, right turn after takeoff, proceed with heading four zero until interecepting the three two five radial from Las Palmas VOR (1706:08.09).

1706:09.61 KLM 4805 – Ah—Roger sir, we are cleared to the Papa Beacon, flight level nine zero until intercepting the three two five. We are now (at takeoff) (1706:17.79)

1706:18.19 Tower – OK...Stand by for takeoff, I will call you (1706:21.79). Note: A squeal starts at 1706:19.39. The squeal ends at 1706:22.06.

1706:21.92 PAA 1736 – Clipper one seven three six (1709:23.19).

1706:25.47 Tower – Ah—Papa Alpha one seven three six report the runway clear (1706:28.89).

1706:29.59 PAA 1736 – OK, will report when we're clear (1736:30.69).

1706:61.69 Tower – Thank you.

Subsequently, KLM 4805, which had released its brakes to start its takeoff run 20 sec. before this communication took place, collided with the PAA. The control tower received no further communications from PAA 1736, nor from KLM 4805.

There were no eyewitnesses to the collision.

Place of accident

The accident took place on the runway of Tenerife Airport (Los Rodeos) at North 28 deg. 28 min. 30 sec latitude and West 16 deg. 19 min. 50 sec. longitude. The field elevation is 2073 ft (632 meters).

Date: The accident occurred on March 27, 1977 at 17 hr. 06 min. 50 sec GMT.

Injuries to persons: KLM 4805 airplane - Fatal: Crew, 14; passengers, 234.

PAA 1736 airplane - Fatal: crew, 9; passengers, 317. Non-fatal: crew 7, passengers 61: others 2. Nine of these passengers died subsequently as a result of injuries received. The others were company employees, sitting on the cockpit jumpseats, who had boarded the plane in Tenerife.

Damage to the aircraft: Damage to the plane was 100% due to the impact and post-impact fire.

Other damage: The runway was damaged in the area of the impact by the impact itself and by the subsequent fire. Costs of the repairs thereof amounted to 16,005,464.22 pesetas.

The following is partial crew information.

KLM Crew:

Captain Jacob Louis Veldhyzen van Zamten, 50. Starting with a private pilot's license issued Dec. 21, 1947, he was type rated in eight commercial aircraft with total flying time of 11.500 hours, with 1545 hours in a 747.

Copilot (First Officer) Klass Meurs, 42, with a private pilot's license issued May 31, 1953, was type rated in 4 commercial aircraft. His total flying time on March 27, 1977 was 9200 hours with 95 hours in a 747. At one time he was a student of Van Zamten.

Flight Engineer Willem Schreuder, 52, with a private pilot's license issued June 10, 1970, but held a flight engineers license dated May 12, 1950. He was type rated in 5 commercial aircraft with 17.031 total flight hours including 543 hours on the 747.

PAA Crew:

Captain Victor F. Grubbs, 56, with rating in 707 and 747 commercial aircraft. His total flying time was 21.043 hours with 564 hours on the 747.

Copilot (First Officer) Robert L. Bragg, 39, with rating in 707 and 747 commercial aircraft. His total flying time was 10.800 hours with 2796 hours on the 747.

Flight Engineer George Warns, 46, with a flight engineer rating in turbojets. His total flying time was 15.210 hours with 559 hours on the 747.

Fire Department action

Alarm and mobilization of the firefighting team. The weather conditions, with fog patches at zero meters prevented the accident from being immediately and directly visible from the control tower, where they only heard one explosion followed by another, without being able to localize them or ascertain their cause.

Moments later, an aircraft located on the parking apron advised the tower that it had seen a fire, without specifying the exact place or its cause.

The tower immediately sounded the fire alarm for the fire service, informing them that there was a fire and that they should be prepared for an urgent departure. The tower had not yet been able to locate the fire.

Subsequently, a member of the CEPSA Co. arrived at the fire station parking lot, where the firemen were all ready and prepared, and told them that there was a fire "to the left of the parking area."

This was the first, though vague, indication regarding the location of the fire. The firemen immediately communicated this information to the tower, and set out at greatest possible speed, which nevertheless was very low on account of the weather conditions which carried the serious risk of collision with persons, vehicles and airplanes, in view of the fact that they had to cross the very congested parking apron diagonally.

Finally, they saw a bright light through the fog and when they came closer, although they were not yet able to see the flames, they suffered the effects of strong heat radiation.

When there was a slight clearing, they saw for the first time that there was an airplane totally engulfed in flames, the only visible part being the rudder.

After they had begun to fight the fire, a greater clearing in the fog took place and they saw a bright light farther away, which they thought at first was part of the same airplane which had also broken off and was also burning.

They divided up the fire trucks and, on approaching what they thought was only a second focal point of the same fire, they discovered a second airplane was on fire. They immediately concentrated their efforts on this second airplane because the first was totally unrecoverable.

As a result of this action, they were able—in spite of the tremendous rage of the fire in this second airplane—to save the left side, from which between 15,000 and 20,000 kilos of fuel were subsequently removed.

Meanwhile, because of the dense cloud surrounding it, the tower was still unaware of the exact location of the fire, and whether one or two airplanes were involved in the accident.

The impact, start of and extinguishing of the fire:

There is no indication of any failure prior to the impact. The distance from the approach end of Runway 30 to the Pan Am wreckage was about 1385 meters. From here to the main KLM wreckage was a distance of about 450 meters.

The Pan Am was at an angle of about 45 deg. relative to the center of the runway, ie at about 75 deg. magnetic. It is possible that it continued to move after the impact.

Apparently, the KLM No. 1 engine only grazed the tip of Pan Am's right side; the nose and landing gear overshot the latter airplane and the main landing gear smashed against it in the area of the No. 3 engine.

The KLM was entirely airborne when the impact took place. Its taildrag had scraped the runway in an excessive rotation for a distance of 65 feet; the tracks on the runway began about 300 ft. before the place of impact.

Some sections of the right side of the Pan Am were found near the KLM, indicating that indeed there was an impact there.

The KLM fuselage skidded over the Pan Am aft fuselage, destroying it and shearing off the empennage. The KLM continued in flight, hitting the ground about 150 meters farther on and sliding another 300 meters on the runway. It caught fire suddenly and violently.

The four available turret trucks, with their corresponding crews, initially were used for extinguishing the fire. Later, all airport fire service vehicles, except one that was out of service and the two first-aid Land Rovers, were added. Likewise, within a few minutes, firefighting units from La Laguna and Tenerife joined in, with three tank trucks. The fire was totally extinguished at 3:30 am on Mar 28.

Five thousand kilos of foam (Tutogene) and about 500.000 liters of water were used in order to put out the fire.

Rescue and survival

There were no survivals in the KLM aircraft, even though the impact against both the Pan Am and the ground could not have been excessively violent; however, an immediate and raging fire must have prevented adequate emergency operations because all of the aircraft's evacuation doors remained shut even though the fuselage was not deformed significantly.

In the Pan Am aircraft, the first class lounge disappeared as a result of the impact, as well as nearly the whole of the top of the fuselage. The lounge floor gave way, which meant that the crew had to jump to the first-class section and get out through a hole in the left wall, behind the L.1 exit. This hole was the main escape route for the passengers located in the forward part of the aircraft. None of those in the first class lounge survived.

According to survivors, the shock of the impact was not excessively violent, leading them to believe that the cause was an explosion. They jumped to the ground through openings in the left side, or through door L.2, which was duly opened, from a height of 20 ft. (6 meters). The left engine was still turning, and there was a fire under the wing at this side. A large number of passengers escaped off this wing, jumping from it to the grass. Explosions were already taking place, and the ambulances appeared almost immediately. At the center and the aft of the plane, the accumulation of wreckage and twisting of metal sheets of the fuselage must have been that, apart from the fire which suddenly broke out, it formed a kind of trap, preventing forward exit of the passengers.

Total evacuation time is estimated to have been about one minute.

The crew and "extra crew" helped effectively in the evacuation. Subsequently, airport personnel and even private individuals who happened to be there also provided effective help.

There were five ambulances in the airport at the time of the accident.

The general plan of evacuation worked very much in accordance with what had been planned in case of an emergency. In general, it was carried out very rapidly, and there was a free traffic flow between the airport and the hospital. This operation was directed by the Civil Guard for Traffic.

Local radio transmitters requested that anyone who could help should go to the airport. This appeal, which undoubtedly was made with the best of intentions, nevertheless had negative consequences because, when most of the people arrived, the PAA injured had already been evacuated, and a traffic jam occurred which could have made the providing of further help more difficult.

There were large scale blood donations. All of the injured were promptly and duly taken care of in the Santa Cruz hospitals, so that it was not necessary to make use of the three surgical teams and 89 hospital beds made available in Puerto do la Cruz.

Socio-psychological causes

Until a few years ago the flight captain was able, at his own discretion, to extend the limit of his crew's activities in order to complete the service. However, this was changed recently in the sense of imposing absolute rigidity with regard to the limit of activity. The captain is forbidden to exceed it and, in case he should do so, may be prosecuted under the law.

Moreover, until December of 1976, it was very easy to fix said limit of activity by taking only a few factors into account, but this calculation has now been made enormously complicated and in practice it is not possible to determine it in the cockpit; for this reason it is strongly recommended that the company should be contacted in order to determine it.

This was the situation in Tenerife, and for this reason Capt. Veldhuyzen (Van Zanten) spoke by HF [radio] to his company's operation office in Amsterdam. There they told him that if he was able to take off before a certain time it would seem that there would be no problems, but that if there was a risk of exceeding the limit they should send a Telex to Las Palmas.

Other possible causes

Route and pilot-instruction experience:

Although the captain had flown for many years on European and intercontinental routes, he had been an instructor for more than 10 years, which relatively diminished his familiarity with route flying. Moreover, on simulated flights, which are so customary in flying instruction, the training pilot normally assumes the role of controller—that is he issues takeoff clearances. In many cases no communications whatsoever are used in simulated flights, and for this reason takeoff takes place without clearance.

Authority in the cockpit:

Although nothing abnormal can be deduced from the CVR, the fact exists that a copilot not very experienced with 747s was flying with one of the pilots of greatest prestige in the company who was, moreover, KLM's chief flying instructor and who had certified him fit to be a crewmember for this type of airplane. In case of doubt, these circumstances could have induced the copilot not to ask any questions, assuming that his captain was always right.

Part B

The following is Part B of the official Spanish Ministry of Aviation and Commerce report on the accident in Tenerife on March 27, 1977. (I did not use all of this report.) This report contains all of the cockpit conversations in addition to the radio transmissions. The Cockpit Voice Recorder [CVR] records all of the conversations in the cockpit. Those are critical to understanding why and how this accident occurred.

Analysis:

On March 27, 1977, a bomb exploded in the terminal building of Las Palmas Airport (Canary Islands), and for this reason the passenger terminal was evacuated. As there had been a threat of a second explosion, much of the traffic arriving at Las Palmas Airport was diverted to that of Los Rodeos on Tenerife Island. For this reason, the parking area at the latter airport was saturated with planes.

The KLM Boeing 747, PH-BUF, arrived at Los Rodeos Airport at 13:38 and was parked at the end of the taxi runway next to a Braathens Boeing 737 (SAFE). Subsequently, a Sterling Boeing 727, a SATA DC-8 and the Pan American 747 N1736, were parked in the same area.

The Pan Am Boeing 747 which arrived at Los Rodeos Airport at approximately 14:15 was parked on the taxi runway next to the above mentioned Braathens Boeing 737, Sterling Boeing 727, SATA DC-8 and the KLM 747, PH-BUF, which arrived at Los Rodeos at 13:38.

Once the Las Palmas Airport had been reopened, the Pan Am plane, N1736, called the tower requesting permission to start up its engines: in reply, it was told that there was no ATC delay, but that they could have problems taxiing on account of the KLM plane which was ahead of it, and that taxiing on the taxiway would not be possible on account of the aircraft congestion on the main apron.

Indeed, when the time came to taxi, the Pan Am was forced, on account of the position of the KLM, which was blocking its way, to wait for the latter's departure. The three other planes parked there had already departed.

Approximately 1 hr. later, KLM 4805 requested an estimated departure time. They said that they needed to refuel and that this would take approximately 30 min. They filled up with 55,500 L while the passengers remained on board. Later, the KLM requested permission to start up its engines, and then clearance to taxi.

It was cleared to taxi toward the holding position of Runway 12 and to change its surface frequency to 118.7 to the approach frequency of 119.7.

A few minutes later, Pan Am called again to request clearance to start up its engines, and was cleared to do so.

If we keep in mind that the Tenerife-Las Palmas flight is one of about 25 min. duration, the taking on of 55,500 L of fuel leads us to suppose that the KLM captain thereby wished to avoid the difficulties of refueling in Las Palmas, with the resulting delay, because a great number of airplanes diverted from Tenerife would be going there later. The aircraft could, in fact, return to Amsterdam with the fuel it had without refueling in Las Palmas.

The conversations which took place between KLM 4805 and the control tower until the plane started to taxi on the main runway were as follows:

The times are those taken from the KLM CVR.

1658:14.8 – KLM 4805 – Approach KLM four eight zero five on the ground in Tenerife.

1658:21.5 – APP – KLM—ah—four eight zero five roger.

1658:25.7 – KLM 4805 – We require backtrack on one two for takeoff runway three zero.

1658.30.4 – APP – OK, four eight zero five…taxi…to the holding position runway three zero taxi into the runway and—ah—leave runway (third) to your left.

1658:47.4 – KLM-4805 – Roger sir (entering) the runway at this time and the first (taxiway) we, we go off the runway again for the beginning of runway three zero.

1658:53.3 – APP – OK. KLM eight zero—correction, four eight zero five taxi straight ahead—ah—for the runway and—ah—make—ah—backtrack.

1659:04.5 – KLM – roger make a "backtrack".

1659:10.0 – KLM 4805 – KLM four eight zero five is now on the runway.

1659:15.9 – APP – four eight zero five roger.

1659:28.4 – KLM 4805 – Approach, you want us to turn left at Charlie one, taxiway Charlie one?

1659:32.28 – APP – Negative, negative taxi straight—ah—up to the end of the runway and make "backtrack".

1659:39.9 – KLM 4805 – OK, sir.

At 1703:14.4, KLM 4805 asked the tower if the runway center lights were in service because, as the weather conditions were becoming worse, he wished to have this information with the minimum required takeoff conditions.

At 1704:58.7, the tower controller, after having checked, replied that the runway centerline lights were out of service, while he also passed this information along to the PAA Clipper 1736.

At 1705:27.08 KLM 4805, which was already at the approach end of Runway 30, completed the turn in order to face in the direction for takeoff. From this point on, the KLM 4805 and the Clipper 1736 CVR tapes, as well as data obtained from the KLM 4805 DFDR (are used) during the last 88 sec.

At 1705:27.98, the engine braking begins and lasts for 2.54 sec.

At 1705:36.7, the copilot finishes the takeoff check list and at 1705:41.22 (67.81 sec. before the impact), a slight forward movement due to opening of the throttle is observed (increase of continued EPR in the four engines). At 1705:41.5 the copilot says: "Wait a minute, we don't have ATC clearance." To which the captain replies, "No, I know that, go ahead, ask."

At 1705:44.6, KLM 4805 tells the control tower, "Ah—the KLM four eight zero five is now ready for takeoff, and we're waiting for our ATC clearance." This message ended at 1705:50.77.

This communication was heard in the PAA cockpit.

At 1705:53.41, the controller gave KLM the following ATC instructions:

"KLM eight seven zero five—uh—you are cleared at the Papa Beacon climb to and maintain flight level nine zero...right turn after takeoff proceed with heading zero four zero until intercepting the three two five radial from Las Palmas VOR." The message ended at 1706:08.9. At the 1706:07.33 before the message ended, the aircraft captain said, "Yes." and 44.31 sec. before the impact the No. 3 engine and No. 4 engine slightly increased their EPR.

At 1706:09.61, the copilot repeated the ATC instructions given by the tower controller, at the following times and as follows:

1706:09.61 – KLM 4805 (RD 2) – "Ah—roger sir, we are cleared to the Papa Beacon flight level nine zero, right turn out zero four zero until intercepting the three two five. We are now at takeoff."

At 1706:11.08, the copilots' repetition of the ATC instruction ended.

At 1706:11.08 the brakes in the KLM 4805 were released.

At 1706:12.25 the aircraft captain said, "Let's go...check thrust", ending this sentence at 1706:16.11.

The following was ascertained from the DFDR data:

1706:11.70 (37.33 sec. before impact): it was deduced from the LONG that the airplane began to move with longitudinal acceleration.

1706:13.99 (35.04 sec. before impact): The EPRs have risen above the level for idling (1.12-1.12-1.14-1.14).

1706:14.94 (34.09 sec. before impact) the start of change of course was observed from the HEAD.

1706:17.17 (31.86 sec. before impact) from the VANE it can be ascertained that lift had begun. Value reached was 6.8 deg. Airspeed was increasing (46.41). Direction straightened out.

From everything that happened during this time, it is seen that while the first officer was repeating the ATC instructions given by the controller, KLM 4805 had already started its ground run. While at 1706:14.00, moreover, the sound of engines starting to accelerate is observed.

At 1706:18.19 the controller replied to the read-back of his ATC clearance in the following way: "OK," and at 1706:20.08 ie., 1.89 sec. later added: "stand by for takeoff...I will call you." ending said message at 1706:21.79.

During this time, at 1706:19.35, the KLM 4805 takeoff had already been reached and stabilized (1.39 to 1.42).

Simultaneously, in the Pan Am cockpit, on hearing this conversation, the pilot says "No uh", and the copilot says "and we are still taxiing down the runway, the clipper one seven three six."

This communication caused a shrill noise in the KLM cockpit, which started at 1706:19.39 and ended at 1706:22.06.

At 1706:25.47, the tower controller confirmed reception of the Pan Am message in the following way: "Papa Alpha one seven three six report when the runway is clear."

This was audible in the KLM cockpit.

The message ended at 1706:28.89.

At 1706:29.59, the PAA replied "OK will report when we're clear." This reply was audible in the KLM cockpit.

The control tower replied, "Thank you." And then the following sentences were spoken in the KLM cockpit:

1706:32.43 – C3 – "Is he not clear, then?"
1706:34.10 – C1 – "What do you say?"
1706:34.15 – PA – "Yup."
1706:34.70 – C3 – "Is he not clear the Pan American?"
1706:35.70 – C1 – "Oh, yes" (emphatically).

At 1706:43.009 the co-pilot intoned the V, and subsequently on the DFDR PCC the following was observed: a pulling of the control column, with the airplane nose pointing up, 16% of the way back from a 44% forward position and from Pitch 2, airplane nose pointing up.

At m1706:46.04 ie. 2.99 sec. before impact, increased direction toward the right is observed in the HEAD: 1.46 sec. later, a curving of the airplane is seen in the ROLL parameter (ROLL) and 1.54 sec before impact, a roll to the right is observed in the Roll Control wheel Position parameter RWC.

At 1706:47.44 the captain utters an exclamation—the impact takes place shortly afterward.

On listening to the PAA CVR it may be deduced that its crew saw the KLM 9.5 sec. before impact.

From the actions of the Tenerife Control Tower, it may be inferred that their ordering of the KLM to leave the runway by the third taxiway was so that they should leave the main runway as soon as possible and then proceed along the parallel taxiway. This third taxiway was the first by which it was possible to take the airplane off the main runway because access to the parallel taxiway by C-1 and C-2 was not possible on account of aircraft congestion on the parking apron.

Later, in order to make the maneuver easier, the controller chose to order this airplane to continue down the right side of the main runway and at the end… make a 180 deg. turn.

Likewise, he indicated to the PAA that they should leave by the third taxiway. At first there was some confusion regarding the words "first" and "third." But this was finally dispelled because the controller made the following clarification: "The third one, Sir, one, two, three, third one."

The situation deteriorated further when lowering clouds reduced visibility to the point at which neither airplane taxiing on the main runway, nor some of those located in the parking area, were visible from the tower.

It transpires from the careful listening to the KLM CVR that although the cockpit operation was correct and the checklists were adequately kept, there was some feeling of anxiety regarding a series of factors, which were: the time margin remaining to them, to the point of straining the allowable limit of their duty time; the poor and changing visibility, which, especially as runway center lights were not operative, might prevent the possibility of takeoff within the weather limits required by the company; the inconvenience for the passengers, etc. It is also observed that, as the time for takeoff approached, the captain—perhaps on account of all these worries—seemed a little absent from all that was heard in the cockpit. He inquired several times, and after the copilot confirmed the order to backtrack, he asked the tower if he should leave the runway by C-1, and subsequently asked his copilot if he should do so by C-4. On arriving at the end of the runway, and making a 180 deg. turn in order to place himself in the takeoff position, he was advised by the copilot that he should wait as they still did not have an ATC clearance. The captain asked him to request it, which he did, but while the copilot was still repeating the clearance, the captain opened the throttles and started to take off. Then the copilot, instead of requesting takeoff clearance or advising that they did not yet have it, added to his readback: "We are now at takeoff." The tower, which was not expecting the aircraft to take off as it had not given clearance, interpreted the sentence as "We are now at takeoff position." (When the Spanish, American and Dutch investigating teams heard the tower recording together and for the first time, no one, or hardly anyone, understood that this transmission meant they were taking off.) The controller replied: "OK…stand by for takeoff…I will call you." Nor did the Pan Am, on hearing the "We are now at takeoff," interpret it as an unequivocal indication of takeoff. However, in order to make their own position clear, they said, "We are still taxiing down the runway." This transmission coincided with the "Stand by for takeoff…I will call you," causing a whistling sound in the tower transmission and making its reception in the KLM cockpit not as clear as it should have been, even though it did not thereby become unintelligible.

The communication from the tower to the PAA requested the latter to report when it left the runway clear. In the cockpit of the KLM, which was taking off, nobody at first confirmed receiving these communications until the Pan Am responded to the tower's request that it should report leaving the runway with an "OK, we'll report when we're clear." On hearing that, the KLM flight engineer asked: "Is he not clear then?" The captain didn't understand him and he repeated, "Is he not clear that Pan American?" The Captain replied with an emphatic "Yes" and, perhaps influenced by his great prestige, making it difficult to imagine an error of this magnitude on the part of such an expert pilot, both the copilot and the flight engineer had no further objections. The impact took place about 13 sec. later.

From that moment until the next call to the airplanes, the tower took care of the IB-185 and the BX-387 and awaited communication from the Pan Am reporting the "runway clear." It also received information from two airplanes located in the parking area that there was a fire in an undetermined place on the field, sounded the alarm, informed the Firefighting and Health Services, and broadcast the news of the emergency situation: it then called the two airplanes on the runway, not receiving any reply.

~   Chapter 9   ∾

LIST OF SURVIVORS FROM PAN AM

Following is a list of the 74 initial survivors of the Canary Islands Aircraft Accident that occurred on Sunday, March 27, 1977. We lost one of them that night. By the following weekend the number of survivors had dropped to 66 and after six weeks that number was 58. So the number of reported survivors depends upon when that measurement was recorded. All hometowns are in California unless otherwise noted. This list was initially furnished by Pan Am.

Initial survivors and their hometowns

Amador, John; Marina Del Rey
Anderson, Marion; San Diego
Anderson, Dr. Karen; Seattle
Bowman, Richard; El Cerrito
Bowman, Mary; El Cerrito
Brown, Jan; Laguna Hills
Brusco, Cleo; Lake Oswego, Or.
Brusco, Roland; Longview, Wa.
Brusco, Terresa; Longview, Wa.
Combs, John; Haleiwa, Ha.
Combs, Louise; Haleiwa, Ha.
Culbertson, Stephen; Green Valley, Az.
Culbertson, Ruth; Green Valley, Az.
Daniel, Patricia; La Verne
Daniel, Lynda; La Verne
Ellerbrock, Byron; Laguna Hills
Ellerbrock, Grace; Laguna Hills
Fox, Kim; Visalia

Heck, Paul; Laguna Hills
Heck, Floy, Laguna Hills
Holt, Joan Devereau; San Diego
Hess, Edward; Phoenix, Az.
Hopkins, Warren; Northbrook, Il.
Hopkins, Caroline; Northbrook, Il.
Jakoubek, Marianne, Visalia
Kershaw, Dorthea; Borrego Springs
Lamp, Edward; Walnut Creek
Libert, Alta; Hemet
Lord, Isabelle; Long Beach
Magante, Maurice; Sacramento
McGowan, Harold; Laguna Hills
McGowan, Grace; Laguna Hills
Miller, Charles; Escondido
Monde, Anthony; La Mesa
Monde, Isobel; La Mesa
Moore, Bethene; San Francisco
Naik, Jim; Cupertino
Naik, Elfreida; Cupertino
Pinkstaff, Charles; San Diego
Reynolds, Bennet; San Leandro
Reynolds, Madeline, San Leandro
Rich, Pamela; Woodlake
Rideout, Edgar; Alpine
Schlect, Erma, Palm Springs
Simon, Ethel; Los Angeles
Sinnet, Richard; Longview, Wa.
Sinnet, Kay; Longview, Wa.
Sparacino, Stephen; Medford, Or.
Tanemura, Roy; Kelona, B.C.
Tartikoff, Jordan; San Francisco
Tartikoff, Enid; San Francisco
Trumbull, Col. Albert; La Mesa
Trumbull, Florence; La Mesa
Tyzbir, Mario; Laguna Hills
Waldrip, Herbert; Laguna Hills
Waldrip, Lara; Laguna Hills
Walker, Larry; Laguna Hills
Walker, Phyllis; Laguna Hills
Waters, Col. Mervin; Petaluma

Wiley (Alexander), David; Palo Alto
Williams, Norman; Palos Verdes

Author's note:
Isabelle Lord died en route to her home
Col. Mervin Waters died in Tenerife hospital

Pan Am crew member survivors

Grubbs, Victor, Captain; Centerport, Me
Bragg, Robert, First Officer; Howard Beach, N.Y.
Warms, George, Flight Engineer; Blairstown, N.Y.
Kelly, Dorothy, Purser; N.H.
Jackson, Joan, Flight Attendant; Nashville, Tn.
Johnson, Carla, Flight Attendant; New York, N.Y.
Donovan, Suzanne, Flight Attendant; Harrisburg, Pa.
Munillo Rivas, Juan Antonio, Pan Am Crew Chief, Las Palmas; Canary Islands
Cooper, Joe, Observer

~ Chapter 10 ~

SURVIVORS, ON
OUR WAY HOME

I met the Pan Am rep in the lobby of Hotel Mencey and checked out of the hotel. Accompanying us was another young man, slightly younger than I. His was a very sad story. He was married to one of the flight attendants who was killed and was there to identify her body and escort her home to New York. He could not find her. Many of the bodies were torn apart and/or burned to such an extent that visual identification was almost impossible. So he was on his way back home without a shred of closure. He was also, surprisingly, very interested to hear my story of the accident. I told him that the smoke and heat from the ensuing fire would have meant a relatively pain free death. The people in the back of the plane, behind the wings, had no chance of survival at all. The KLM 747 had sheared the whole back end off the Pan Am plane. They may have seen a puff of smoke but then it was all over for them. He was not sure where her assigned location was on the plane. But he could not find her now.

We got in a cab and headed to the airport. Inside the terminal there were no passengers. It was eerily empty as the airport was closed to all air traffic. Several people were standing at an oval desk and I recognized one of them. It was the doctor who had examined me and helped to triage patients in the hospital. He was on his way home with several other doctors who had flown over from New York to help the many wounded survivors. I walked over and spoke with him briefly. He asked about my head wound and I replied that my head was hard as a rock and the wound would be fine! I believe that another person standing at the counter was the Pan Am ground crew chief from Las Palmas, Juan Antonio Munillo Rivas. We shook hands and we three travelers were on our way again. We walked downstairs and out onto the tarmac and boarded a helicopter.

The helicopter was the only air transport to or from Tenerife. The wreckage of the burned 747s had closed the main runway because it was badly damaged by the impact points and heat from the fires. The helicopter was painted a bright orange and was the kind with the cockpit above and ahead of the passenger cabin. We climbed in and closed the sliding door. The engine started up and we were off. That was my first time in a helicopter. The seating was along each side wall and the seatbelts kept us from sliding around.

We were soon over open water. It was a beautiful sight. I was taking in all the sights and sounds of this flight when we got a big surprise. The sliding door flew open, sliding back to reveal an even better view of the ocean! I tightened my seat belt a little more and looked at my fellow passengers. We just stayed in our seats as we were in no real danger there. I wasn't really scared as I felt that I was inde-structible at that time. I just survived the worst aviation accident in world history. What more could be done to me? We landed at Las Palmas near the terminal. We walked by the front of the helicopter and I stopped and saluted the flight crew. I was pleased to be on my way home.

However, there was a delay. As our Pan Am escort told us, we might not get to Las Palmas in time to catch the flight to London, my intermediate stop. We did indeed miss that flight and stayed in a hotel in Las Palmas. We were instructed to meet for breakfast early for a flight north.

Wednesday morning dawned early for us. After breakfast we headed for the airport. My fellow traveler was booked on a separate flight so I wished him well on his journey home to New York. I was booked on TAP airlines to Lisbon, Portugal with an intermediate stop in Madera, a Portuguese island north of the Canary Islands. That was also one of the ports of call of the cruise I had planned to see. In Lisbon I would change planes to British Airways and continue to London with a stop in Porta, Portugal.

The airport on Madera has an interesting layout and an odd runway. It's not straight. About a third of the way down the runway there is a slight turn to the left. Also, it's built into the side of a cliff next to the ocean with a 600 foot drop off on three sides. On the inland side is a cut through a low hill to the airport itself. Igno-rance is bliss which was helpful to me at the time as I was unaware of this situation. (Several months later a jetliner on final approach to Madera landed short and in the water. I don't believe there were fatalities). After a short layover in Madera we continued on to Lisbon. A Pan Am rep met me at the front door and escorted me to the gate for my continuation flight on British Airways to London. That flight was a little odd as well. As we touched down in Porta, Portugal, the plane slammed into the runway and bounced hard. (The plane was a British made Trident, similar to the Boeing 727 with three engines in the tail.) After a short turnaround we were airborne again bound for London. The landing there was a hard slam as well. That was very strange and a little unnerving.

Upon deplaning in London a Pan Am agent met me at the door and escorted me to a hotel. (That was Dave Samson, director of passenger services, UK and Western Europe. I still have his card in my scrapbook). The flight was the next day as we missed the Wednesday flight. The plan was to board another Pan Am 747 for San Francisco, with a stop in Seattle. I have relatives in Seattle so I thought that might be fun. Sometimes nothing is easy for me and so it was with the final flight home.

The Pan Am service rep, Dave Samson, called me early the next morning, Thursday, March 31. He said there was a problem with one of the engines on the 747 that was to take me home to San Francisco. One of the engines would not start. A crew of mechanics was working on it but then they would have to test it. Dave suggested I might as well stay at the hotel until we got a firm takeoff time. Five hours later we were ready to go. (The flight crew tested the engine by initiating a full takeoff run, without passengers, then aborting the takeoff. The engine came up to full power and they were satisfied with the engine's performance.)

Dave met me in the hotel lobby and escorted me to the gate. That was a little tricky because I did not have a passport. My passport had been in the camera bag under the seat in front of me on Clipper Victor. But with my driver's license and an escort, I had no problem boarding any of the flights. On this flight Pan Am put me in a seat on the right side of the lower first class cabin. That was cool!

I was settling into my seat while the other passengers boarded the plane. I was sort of spacing out, relaxing when I heard a female voice say "Hello David." I was surprised and looked up to see one of the other walking survivors. It was Marion Anderson of San Diego, California. I was happy to see her! Because of the five hour delay in our departure time, she was able to make this flight. We chatted for a while, then took our seats. We took off soon thereafter without incident.

There was another survivor on this flight. She was badly banged up with cuts and bruises and did not want to talk very much. Later on during the flight the man who was sitting next to her talked to me as I was stretching my legs. The injured woman was Dr. Karen Andersen of Seattle. The couple with her were her parents. He and his wife had flown to Tenerife to escort Karen back to Seattle. He told me that Karen's husband, also a doctor, had died in the accident. I was so saddened by that news and wished that I had been more sensitive to her feelings. I became even sadder upon arrival in Seattle. We survivors were asked to wait until all of the other passengers had deplaned. After most of the passengers were off the plane, two small children were escorted on board. They ran to Karen and hugged her. I was in tears as I realized that these were the children of Karen and her late husband. My problems seemed so small then.

About this time an agent with U.S. Immigration and Customs boarded the plane and spoke with us. He was very polite, explaining that he understood our situation but he was required to ask us certain questions. He asked to see our passports. I explained to him that my passport had been in my camera bag under the seat in front of me so I no longer had it. My other photo ID was sufficient and we were cleared to enter the country. The other walking survivor, Marion Anderson, was escorted off the plane and on to her next flight south to San Diego.

I had an hour and a half of free time until the same plane continued on to San Francisco. I was escorted off the plane by a female Pan Am agent who took me to an office where I could use a phone. I have several relatives in the Seattle area. We were walking down an escalator to the lower level when I saw a woman standing in an open area below us. I freaked out! It was my aunt, Norma Lee Labbe, of Seattle. I yelled out something and began running down the escalator focusing on my aunt. I guess my poor escort almost fell down as I took off. As she caught up with us, I introduced them and we headed for an office.

As we walked away, a reporter from the *Seattle Times* approached us and asked me for an interview. I said sure and we chatted for a bit and a photo was taken of my aunt and me. Then Norma Lee and I were escorted to an office where I was allowed to make some calls. I spoke with an uncle from the other side of the family (Norma Lee was my Dad's sister). He knew from my parents that I was one of the survivors of the accident in Tenerife. We chatted for a while and I was feeling pretty good. I said goodbye to my aunt, thanked the Pan Am customer service rep and boarded the Pan Am 747 for the final leg of this long journey home.

I was both nervous and excited as we taxied out for takeoff from SeaTac headed for SFO. I knew that my parents would meet me at the gate. I would be SO happy to see them again. The plane would arrive shortly after 11pm and I was concerned that a contingent of press would be there and bother my parents. So I wrote a note to the purser to call ahead and ask for security at the gate.

The flight itself was pretty wicked. We flew south in to some severe turbulence over Oregon. The plane was rocking back and forth like crazy! I knew that the plane could easily withstand this weather but I became nervous anyway. It got so bad that I had to hold my cup of soda on my table to keep it from spilling. Then the purser announced that they were suspending beverage service until the weather calmed down. Finally, I could see the lights of the Bay Area. We made the big loop from a southern heading into the north position for our final approach over the bay. We "jumped the fence" and landed smoothly. I stayed on board until all the other passengers were off the plane. A gate agent came onboard and escorted me off the plane. I thanked the flight attendants for their service and we headed out the left front door. I noticed two police officers standing in the jetway.

As we walked into the gate area, I saw very few people there and no press at all. We approached a glassed-in room on the right and I saw my parents in there, waiting for me. Also, with them were two of my coworkers, Bob Dippel and Ron Nelson, plus a couple of my neighbors, Clayton and Mrs. Robertson who had given me a ride to the airport to start this trip. The gate agent had difficulty unlocking the door to this room. We were so close but we could not get to each other! So we walked around the corner to the other side and I went inside there. I thanked the gate agent and we were left alone to reunite. I hugged all of them and tears flowed.

The Robertsons brought some mail for me, in case I wanted to go with my parents. Bob brought along an old pair of glasses of mine that I kept in my tool box at work. They were very helpful to have again.

Then they asked me to tell the whole story so I spoke of the fog and the impact once again.

I recounted how I did not see the KLM 747 coming toward us as we turned to the left and how they hit us more on the right side. The plane came to a hard stop and filled with smoke. How something, probably the overhead baggage bin door, fell on top of me and knocked my glasses off. I did not even reach down to get them. With my right arm I threw off whatever had landed on me and as I looked up, I could see blue sky! I whipped off the belt, stood up and turned around. There was a blank spot there in my memory but it seemed that I stepped on the seat, then on the back of the seat, moved some wires out of the way and stepped out of this hole, down a slight slope and onto the right wing. I looked to my right, looking forward, and could not even see the plane because it was completely enveloped in smoke. Flames were arcing around both sides of the cowling of the inboard engine and a woman was lying on the wing. She was wearing a dark blue pantsuit and had white or grey hair. She was lying on her back with her head towards me and I could see her lips moving. She stretched her hands up towards me and she was saying "Help me." As she was sliding forward towards the engine fire, I grabbed her by the wrists and began to pull her. I pulled her back onto the wing a few feet, then turned and pulled her out on the wing to a point between the engines. Then there was another blank spot in my memory. I do not know what I did with her.

As I am standing on the leading edge of the wing, I look down and see green. It's grass. I think I was about twenty feet off the ground. My camera was hanging around my neck and I held it so that it would not fly up and hit me in the face. I jumped off. When I landed I rolled forward and skinned the palms of my hands. At that point, my hearing came back. (I did not hear anything during the impact. Other survivors noticed the same thing). I could hear this loud booming man's voice somewhere out in front of me. He was screaming, "Run. Run. Run." That was our copilot, Bob Bragg, whom I had seen on my tour of the cockpit. I got up and ran. I ran through the tall wet grass that was between the runway and the taxiway. When I got to the taxiway, I stopped and looked back.

Our Pan Am 747 was not burning too badly. Lots of smoke was pouring out of the plane but not many flames. Then I looked to my right and saw the KLM plane 400 yards or more down the runway. Her nose gear had collapsed and the fuselage was cracked open crossways behind the dome so that her nose was touching the ground. The tail section was broken the same way. There was a HUGE fire coming out of the belly of the plane from the area of the main landing gear, which was down and locked. The flames were shooting down to the ground and then flaring up as high as the top of the fuselage. I saw no one moving there.

As I looked back at the Pan Am 747 I focused on the exit door over the wing. I did not see anyone else come out that hole. Then a fireball of flames shot up about 60 feet in the air from near the wingtip. It came down rapidly. Then the wind caught it and blew it against the plane. POOF!! The entire plane lit on fire. I ran farther away, across the taxiway, then I realized that I had my camera with me. Because of my training I knew the importance of documentation. What did it look like? Where was it sitting? After I took the first shot I checked the internal light meter and found that it was too dark. I adjusted the F stop and took four more photos in rapid succession. Then I sat down and began to cry. The story goes on and on from there.

⤝ Chapter 11 ⤜

RETURNING TO THE LIFE I KNEW

I arrived home in Palo Alto, California, on Thursday evening, March 31. After I related my story to my parents and friends at the San Francisco airport, I decided that I wanted to go to my home in Palo Alto. I rode with the Robertsons to our homes in Creekside Trailer Lodge. It was good to be back in my own bed! Someone suggested that I take the phone off the hook so I could sleep, which I did. Almost as soon as I returned the receiver to its cradle, the next morning the phone rang. It was a reporter from the local paper, the *Palo Alto Times*. I said, "Sure, come on over." Soon, the reporter and a photographer were there.

The caption on the paper's story the next day was "I lost everything but me!" The accompanying photo showed me playing my organ. Another shot showed me

hugging my neighbor, Lee Ola.

Playing music on the organ turned out to be excellent therapy. What was the first piece I played that morning? It was "Amazing Grace." Absolutely. "I was lost but now I'm found." I always get teary eyed when I hear it or play it. That hymn is so powerful and universal.

After the reporter left that Friday morning, I called my retired neighbor, Clayton. He felt that I should not drive right away so he offered to drive me around town, wherever I wanted to go. I wanted to go to my workplace to see all of my friends and co-workers. Off we went. First we went to see my doctor for a cursory exam. I brought along the x-rays from Candelario Hospital in Santa Cruz de Tenerife. My GP, Dr. Royce, verified that I did not have a skull fracture and removed the three stitches from my scalp. Then he checked my eyes and did not see anything unusual. The healing process for my minor physical wounds was proceeding nicely.

Then we headed off to Teledyne MEC, my employer, in the Stanford Industrial Park.

As a defense contractor, Teledyne MEC always had security present at all the entrances. It was nice to see our favorite guard on duty as I made my way inside that Friday morning. I went to my production line first, then made my way around the plant.

It was then that I heard about the radio interview that I did with KNBR from my room in Hotel Mencey. At the time it never dawned on me that they taped the conversation. But they did record it and played it on the air. Several of my co-workers heard it and sent word throughout the plant. One of them called the station and asked them to play it again for all of David's co-workers. I was told that when it came on the air again, all work in the plant came to a complete stop. People left their work stations, gathered in groups and listened in total silence. Ringing phones were ignored. Nobody said a word. At the end of the interview, a loud cheer went up throughout the plant! Wow! That must have been a tremendous relief for my friends. And now, everywhere I went in that two-story building, people came out to see me.

Somebody noticed that the jeans I was wearing had blood stains on them. I explained that all of my clothes were in my suitcase on board Pan Am Clipper Victor. My boots had black marks on them. I must have stepped in fire at some point but I had no memory of that. I was so happy to see friends! Even the Teledyne MEC president, Jack Blake, wanted to see me. What a fantastic day that was! That too will always be a part of me.

While I was chatting with Jack Blake, I asked him if he knew of a good civil attorney. He and Vice President Norm Pond readily recommended E. Jerry Berg of Palo Alto. That Friday afternoon I called Jerry's office and made arrangements to see him. I didn't know much about attorneys but I felt that I wanted a person who was near my home.

Jerry was able to see me later that afternoon and we began a relationship that lasted about ten months. I was still running on adrenaline as I explained to Jerry what had happened to me on that fog-enshrouded runway on the island of Tenerife. I really had to stop and think about every detail of the whole experience again. I also needed to tell the story in sequence.

First, Jerry asked me to tell him my story in minute detail. Over the next hour and a half I explained again the wait on the ground in Tenerife, the fog rolling in just as we began to taxi out for takeoff, the impact. I recalled the 747's sudden stop and the smoke and heat of the resulting fire. Jerry took notes in longhand on a tablet as I continued with the part of the story where I walked out onto the left wing and found the woman in the blue pantsuit sliding towards the inboard engine fire. He was especially interested in the details of my jump off the wing and the sudden stop on the ground. I explained that I had pain in my lower back and he referred me to a neurologist for initial treatment. He also referred me to a psychiatrist to help treat the mental anguish that I was experiencing. At first, I protested this referral. The macho man in me insisted that I was OK and did not need counseling. I was wrong, of course. I relented and agreed to meet with the doctor.

I was getting mentally exhausted during this long conversation with Jerry. I had to try to remember every detail about the events leading up to the collision, the impact and fire, my escape and treatment at the hospital. It was all there, in longhand.

I told him about my office visit with my GP earlier that day. The wound on my head was healing nicely. I had some pain in my eyes but the doctor found nothing unusual there.

The other part of my case concerned the photographs that I had taken. They were important to me as I wanted to share them with my friends. I wanted to get them back so my attorney made arrangements to contact an attorney in Holland. I signed an agreement with Jerry, indicating that he was my exclusive representative for this entire case. If anybody asked me any questions about my case, I was to refer them to Mr. Berg. I always carried his card with me.

I learned a lot about attorneys over the next year. I learned that, just like doctors, they are not equally skilled. The size of a settlement in a civil case depends to a large extent upon the individual attorney and his or her track record. So an attorney who is able to negotiate a large settlement develops a reputation that enables him or her to get larger settlements in the future. Jerry was a very good negotiator but did not have an extensive track record of settlements. Still, I liked his attitude and felt comfortable with his representation.

That Saturday afternoon I went to my favorite Mountain View mall and bought several changes of clothing. I bought everything except handkerchiefs as I had bought a set of them at a store in Santa Cruz de Tenerife. The only clothes I had left were the ones I was wearing at the time of impact on Tenerife. I had taken along enough clothes for the two week cruise including my suit for formal affairs on board the ship. Men are lucky with clothes. It's okay to wear the same suit at several functions during a cruise. Women, on the other hand, want a different outfit for every occasion. No wonder they have two or three suitcases for a trip like this!

On Saturday night my friend and co-worker, Bob Dippel and his wife, Kathy, invited me and my other picture-taking co-worker, Ron Nelson, to their house for dinner. That was a nice respite. Their two toddler daughters were happy to see me. I couldn't pick them up because of the pain in my lower back. So I sat down and they crawled up in my lap. It was nice to be around such innocence again.

When I first thought about taking this cruise, I approached Ron about going with me. After a few days he decided that he wanted to do something else with his vacation time. I was SO glad that he decided not to join me.

After dinner I was asked again to recount my story. I told them about taking some photos of the burning Pan Am 747. I can hardly wait to see them, I said. They should be quite impressive. The next day I got a hint of what they looked like.

The next morning the owner of a downtown Palo Alto magazine/book store called me to tell me that my photos had been published on the front page of the *London Sunday Times* newspaper. I drove down there right away. As I stood in the store looking at the top half of the front page at the photo, I was again in shock and disbelief. It was one of my photographs and the caption under it noted my name as the photographer and survivor. The photo showed the Pan Am 747's burning wreckage on the ground of the fog-enshrouded runway on the island of Tenerife, Canary Islands. Seventy seconds before I snapped that picture I was inside that giant airliner. I bought two copies of the newspaper. I began to get the sick feeling that I had been victimized by Hans Hofman.

On that same Sunday, April 2, 1977 the residents of Creekside Trailer Lodge, the mobile home park where I had lived for four years, hosted a potluck picnic for me. All 29 mobile home park spaces plus a permanent house were fully occupied and we all knew each other. Today was a good time to gather in celebration of a second chance at life.

My parents drove down from Ukiah. With them were my brother Dan, ten years younger than I, and my little sister, Cheryl, who is thirteen years younger. My other sister, Marcia, three years younger than I, was married and lived in Missoula, Montana, at that time. I spoke with her on the phone later that night.

That afternoon I learned what this ordeal had been like for my siblings.

Cheryl had been doing homework in the living room while watching TV. The regular programming was interrupted to announce that there had been an aircraft accident on the island of Tenerife in the Canary Islands. Two 747s had collided and there were many casualties. Cheryl dashed out to the covered patio in back of the house. She told our parents what she had heard. They all came back inside and listened intently to what was being said on TV.

Before I left on this trip I was so excited about it that I had written Cheryl with many cruise details. It included the Pan Am flight number, 1477. Cheryl wondered if that could be the plane I was on? Shortly, the news media reported that the 747s were operated by KLM and Pan Am. At that point, my mother called the Pan Am office at San Francisco International Airport (SFO). The customer service representative was very helpful and kept my parents informed as soon as there was any information. They confirmed that this was indeed a charter flight booked by Royal Cruise Lines flying to Las Palmas, Canary Islands from Los Angeles International Airport (LAX). They also stated that there was no list of survivors yet.

My mother felt that if I had died that it was an instant death but that if I had somehow survived, I got out of the plane without a scratch. She was almost right.

Late that Sunday afternoon Bob Dippel called my parents. He had heard the news as well and wanted to know what my parents knew. Mother relayed the latest information from Pan Am and promised to keep him informed. The news became grim as the afternoon turned into evening. More than 500 people had died in the collision, including all of the passengers on the KLM 747. My parents wondered, what was the chance that their son had survived this horrendous accident when so many people had died?

As the 11 o'clock news came on the TV, an initial list of survivors and their hometowns were posted. My name was the first one on the list! My last name was misspelled but my parents knew it was me! The euphoria and relief must have been incredible. A few moments later the phone rang again. It was Pan Am who confirmed what was posted on the late night TV news. A few moments after that, the phone rang again. It was me!

I told Mom that I was alright but there was a problem with the airplane. They knew that already. The accident in Tenerife was the first item on the evening and late news. My co-worker, Bob, had just called and she planned to call him right back with the good news. I added that I lost my glasses during the impact so I couldn't read very well. I told her I had three stitches in the rear right side of my head. She asked, thirty? No, Mom, just three, I replied.

My brother Dan said that right away the next day and evening, the phone started ringing and just rang and rang for a long time. Dan sat in a tall chair in the kitchen next to the phone and kept answering it and jotting down the names of the callers. Ukiah was a fairly small town of about 12,000 people where my father had been the minister of the First Christian Church during the four years that I was in high school, until the fall of 1966. Now he worked for the Mendocino County Welfare Department, Child Services Division, as a social worker.

The potluck picnic at Creekside Trailer Lodge that day was a delight! All of my neighbors were there plus my family. We took lots of pictures that day. At some point during the gathering I went to my home, which was just across the driveway from where we were picnicking. I left the door open and turned on my organ. I'm sure I started to play with "Amazing Grace" and then played one or two more popular songs. When I went back to the picnic, my Dad said that it was SO good to hear me play again.

My phone rang during the lunch and I ran inside to answer it. The man on the line said that he was Jaap Visering, editor of a small Dutch magazine called *Niewe Review*. Hans Hofman had given him copies of my photos for publication. Editor Visering asked me for my address so he could send me a copy of that issue. I complied and asked him to send two copies of the magazine, one for me and one for my parents. He said that Hans would send copies of the photos to me as well. That was my second notice that the photos had been published.

As the potluck picnic was winding down, a van drove up. Inside were a re-porter for the local NBC TV station and a cameraman. I had agreed to do an interview based on an earlier phone call. We sat in chairs on the lawn where the lunch had been and I retold most of my story about the impact of the two 747s and my escape off the left wing of the Pan Am jumbo jet. I got a picture of us before they gathered up their equipment. Most of my neighbors gathered their items as well and headed home. My parents and siblings headed back to Ukiah. I promised them that I would drive up there for a visit soon. As I watched them drive away, I wondered what Monday would bring.

I stayed home that week, the second week of my planned vacation. My doctor wanted me to rest. My attorney wanted to see me again and plan out my case fur-ther. So that worked out well.

My attorney met with me early in the week. He referred me to a specialist, a neurologist, Dr. Perlstein, about the shooting pain in my lower back. I could not stand up nor sit down for more than 15 minutes at a time. The doctor took a look at my lower back and quickly diagnosed the problem as a bruised right sacroiliac joint. He explained that the sacroiliac is a horseshoe-shaped bone structure at the bottom of the back which supports the entire upper body. At the bottom of this structure are the left and right joints which are connected to the legs. Each joint has a cushion of tissue that protects the bone and nerve endings. My right joint cushion was bruised by the sudden stop when I jumped off the burning plane's wing. A poor solution would be to put me in traction for three months after which I would need to relearn how to walk. Being a practical person, he opted to have me wear a back brace to add extra support to my lower back, strengthen it and reduce the pain. I hoped it would work.

About two weeks after the accident I was invited to the San Francisco office of Royal Cruise Lines. Two of my co-walking survivors, Enid Tartikoff and Jim Naik (the RCL chief financial officer) were employed there and they invited me to join them for lunch during the week. I had sent a copy of my outline to Enid. It was good to see them. (Jim's wife, Elfie, had been burned in the accident and spent three months in a local hospital near San Jose, California. Enid's husband, Jordan had an injured finger but was otherwise unhurt, physically.)

During lunch with many of Enid Tartikoff's co-workers, one of them pointed out the outline that I had written. They were glad that I had written down my memories of that series of events that changed my life forever. Seeing the short sentences made the event seem real to them. I'm sure that all the survivors were in sensory overload condition at the time. Just a few words here and there helped to jog their memories to fill in some of the blank spaces. One of Enid's co-workers told me that he wept when he read my notes. Even though he had heard other firsthand accounts of the accident, reading the outline had really brought it home for him.

Before lunch, co-survivor Jim Naik told me that 114 bodies from our plane still had not been identified. He explained that the medical examiner in Tenerife had some help from the U.S. but they still were having trouble with the identification process. In some cases there were incomplete bodies or just parts of bodies which made identification difficult. The cruise line provided names and seat assignments but trying to identify an individual was, in some cases, almost impossible. This was a time before DNA processes were well defined so most identification was through dental records. I remember seeing a photo in a European magazine that showed this process underway. It was shot from high up on a ladder inside an airplane hangar. Hundreds of caskets were resting on the saw horses that filled this hangar. They were arranged in neat rows. Men in white coats could be seen at places around the floor going about their grim task. That was a stark visualization of the number of casualties from this tragic accident. It was important to provide closure to the families of those who died.

Several times in the two or three months after the accident I experienced severe pain in my eyes again. The pain would occur when I was asleep. When I tried to open my eyes, I had a terrible pain in my eyes. When this happened during the first night after the accident on March 27, I thought that perhaps the pain was related to crying so much. Sometimes the focus of my eyes would change. After an hour or two my normal focus would return. During the first cursory visit with my GP doctor, Dr. Royce, he looked into my eyes and found no injury or foreign object. I finally mentioned this problem to my attorney. I was gently chastised for not mentioning this problem before as this was an injury sustained in the aircraft accident.

I was referred to an ophthalmologist, Dr. Ballin, at the Palo Alto Medical Clinic. He looked at my eyes under a microscope and found numerous cuts across the surface of both eyes. Dr. Ballin explained that during sleep time the eyes normally dry out. In my case the new cells that grew in the cuts on the surface of my eyes would become attached to my eyelids. When I opened my eyes the new cells were being ripped out of the surface of my eyes. The pain was incredibly intense! Dr. Ballin explained that this was a fairly common problem and the treatment was simple. I was to insert a jelly-like ointment into my eyes at bedtime. That would keep my eyes moist during sleep time and the cuts would heal after two months or so. That sounds simple enough to most people but I had a real problem with the treatment. I have very sensitive eyes and have a hard time with even eye drops being dribbled into my eyes. How on Earth was I going to push an ointment into my eyes? With mind over matter and perseverance I was able to treat myself with this healing ointment. I had no more eye pain after that. During my follow up visit with Dr. Ballin he found that all of the cuts in both eyes had healed successfully. I was so happy!

∂⁄ Chapter 12 ⁄∂

BACK TO WORK

In mid-April of 1977 I went back to work. It felt good to be back among my coworkers and do meaningful work. By doctors' orders I was not allowed to lift anything over ten pounds. That's not much weight and it limited some of the work I could perform. Tuning and testing the microwave amplifiers was not a problem. I was performing the final test phase of production. My co-worker weighed a Travelling Wave Tube amplifier and we found that it was well under ten pounds. I could easily connect them to the test stand and remove them after final test. I was back in the groove of the final test process and could get products out the door to our customers.

However, I was also involved with test equipment that needed calibration by moving it to and from the Instrument Calibration and Repair Lab. All of the equipment used in the test of a product had to be calibrated and most of the equipment weighed more than ten pounds. Each item had a calibration sticker on it noting the calibration date and the due date for recalibration. Production came to a screeching halt if any test equipment was overdue for calibration. We had some backup equipment but one of my jobs was to make sure that all of our equipment was up to date. Somebody else took over that function for a while.

Concentration on the work at hand was a big help to my recovery. The biggest help, though, came from the Palo Alto psychiatrist, Dr. Richard Rawson, referred by Jerry Berg. I was traumatized from the near death experience of being inside a jetliner, on the ground, when it was torn apart and caught on fire. I feared being trapped inside an enclosed space, unable to escape the fire.

Fear of heights was less of a trauma but still there was the trauma of standing on the wing of that 747 while it was on fire and deciding what to do. Do I jump or burn? (I had very little hesitation.)

He used light hypnosis to bring out suppressed memories of the accident. Suppressed memories are those images that are in one's subconscious mind. We are unaware of them but they can surface in dreams or other ways and cause distress. I was especially concerned about what I saw when I turned around after I stood up after the impact. What did I see as I looked towards the rear of the plane as it had been torn off by the impact? What did I do with the woman on the wing? Under hypnosis, he determined that there were no suppressed memories of those events so there would not ever be nightmares with those images. There was no filling in the blank spots in my memory. He explained that sometimes images that the mind sees are so horrible that the mind does not record them so there is no memory of them.

The other trauma that we discussed was my being victimized by the man I call the "Fat Dutchman." Hans Hofman took advantage of me while I was in a very weak emotional state. I had lost control of MY photographs and someone else was making money off them.

After the therapy sessions with Dr. Rawson began, I found that some of my physical pain began to diminish. I had learned in a classroom about the connection between emotional distress and physical pain but at the time I doubted that it was real. I became a believer! Emotional distress does indeed cause and extend physical pain.

My attorney and I hoped that Dr. Rawson's final report would help my case by detailing my injuries. His report was not as helpful as we had hoped. Dr. Rawson explained to me that he did not want to get involved as a witness for the plaintiff in a proposed lawsuit arising out of this accident. He was quite willing to write a report on my condition, however. The resulting letter was sent to my attorney and it was quickly determined that the letter was not all that helpful to my case. We expected a stronger case for mental anguish but we did not get that from Dr. Rawson.

However, in his defense, I believe that the treatment provided by Dr. Rawson was very helpful in my emotional recovery from the aircraft accident. I did not have any nightmares about the accident after his treatment sessions.

One of the soothing things I did soon after my return to work was to write down some of the details of the accident. At home one morning I wrote an outline of about three pages and took it with me to work, as I started my afternoon swing shift. I made some copies of it and posted a copy on the bulletin board in the cafeteria. I walked by later and noticed that it was gone. I went through that process several more times. I found that my coworkers were so interested in my notes that they took the outline with them and forgot to put it back. They were hungry for information and I gave it to them.

About six weeks after the accident a woman who supported my production line with order processing services left word that she wanted to see me. When I saw her she explained that she had read an article in the *San Jose Mercury* newspaper about a couple from San Diego who had also survived the aircraft accident. The article stated that the couple was sitting in Row 30. I was astounded! I was sitting in that same row in seat 30C and was not aware of any survivors around me. At that time I understood that no one had survived in the plane farther back than Row 9, except me in Row 30. My coworker promised to bring in the clipping the next day.

I anxiously approached my coworker's desk the next afternoon at the start of my swing shift. She opened the newspaper clipping and gave it to me. "They're alive! They're alive!" I exclaimed! Then I began to weep. The people in the accompanying photograph were Florence and Albert Trumbull, the 71-year-old newlyweds from San Diego. They were sitting in seats 30D and 30E, right across the aisle from me. The couple who traded those seats for Albert and Florence's originally assigned seats four or five rows ahead were killed. That trade made the difference between life and death.

The next morning I got on the phone with an operator and was able to contact Florence and Albert. They indeed remembered me and were looking for me. They wanted to thank me for helping them survive the accident. I told them that my recollection of the moments after impact had blank spots. Florence was able to help fill in some of those spots. She said that right after the impact they looked up to their left and saw me go out a hole in the fuselage, above the seats by the window and they followed me. She told me that the ceiling came down to a point below the top of the seats right next to me and crushed the couple who was sitting there. They died on impact. There was nothing I could have done for them. Then I heard some good news.

Florence told me that another couple (Byron and Grace Ellerbrock) who were sitting on the far side of the section in seats 30F and 30G had also survived the accident! They followed Florence and Albert Trumbull out of the plane. Florence pointed out an article that Grace had written for *Family Circle* magazine about the accident. (I have that in my extensive scrapbook too). I was totally amazed! Those four people had survived the worst aviation accident in world history because they chose to follow me out of the burning wreckage!

In fact, one of those four people wanted to wait for the fire truck but their spouse said no. Florence provided me with the Ellerbrocks' phone number and I called them as well. It was then that I realized that they were the four survivors, in a photograph, lying on the ground in front of the burning wreckage. One of the flight attendants is bent over speaking with them. I think her name is Carla Johnson. One of the male survivors in that photo is walking away from the camera with most of his clothing burned off.

That photograph was one of several taken by a local native of Tenerife, and published in the United States. The credit line reads: MANUAL FANDINO – KAPPA – LIASON. Kappa and Liason are photo agencies that buy and sell photos to the news media. Somehow, possibly from the cruise line, I heard that the other photographer, whom I now believe to be Manuel Fandino, had never seen a Boeing

747 before. Hearing that there were two of them at the airport he drove over to take some photos. When the fog cleared he got much more than he expected. I believe that he is the one who took the photo of me, standing there with my camera around my neck, reaching into my rear pocket to retrieve my handkerchief to wipe the blood off the side of my head. He and I were the only photographers on hand to document the carnage. His photos were the ones published in the United States.

Chapter 13

SECOND CHANCE AT
A HAPPY LIFE

In May of 1977, I went to a boat show at the fairgrounds in San Jose, at the south end of San Francisco Bay. My desire to be out on the water never left me. That's why I had really enjoyed taking the 1976 Caribbean cruise.

I started to get serious about buying my own boat not long after the aircraft accident. I went to a couple of marinas just north of Palo Alto in Redwood City. I looked at a couple of used boats but found nothing that stoked my interest. My back pain was very much an issue in deciding what kind of boat to get. My observation was that a sailboat required a lot of pulling on lines to raise the sails and tack or turn the boat. That would put a lot of strain on my lower back so a sailboat was not an option.

The boat would have to be a power boat. All I would have to do was push up the throttles and away I would go. I felt that I would know what boat model I wanted when I saw it. It happened at the South Bay Boat Show. Of all the power boats in the main display arena this one spoke to me. It was a 24-foot Reinell, with a flying bridge, which means it had seating and another steering station above the main cabin. I spoke with the salesperson who also owned the dealership. I returned that night with a deposit check and signed the paperwork. That particular boat had already been sold so I would get the next one off the production line. My boat would be white with yellow trim. Once I saw the actual boat I came up with a name for her. She would become Grand Canary. The name certainly had a double meaning for me. The dealer worked with me to get a slip in Docktown Marina in Redwood City and he delivered the boat to the ramp at the marina on Fourth of July weekend. I was excited and scared at the same time!

It was very windy on the Saturday afternoon the boat was delivered. An employee of the boat dealership started the Ford 351 V8 engine that was connected to a Volvo outdrive. After he made sure the engine did not overheat, he drove it, at my request, with me aboard, into my assigned slip. I was very excited to have the boat at my disposal but I was too nervous, because of the wind speed, to take her out on my own for the first time. I spent the rest of the afternoon checking out the systems on board and taking some pictures of her.

I also met the nearby neighbors. Bill and Mary Baker also had a Reinell power boat. As we became acquainted I mentioned that I was one of the survivors of the aircraft accident on Tenerife in the Canary Islands. They became visibly shaken. Bill explained that they had booked passage on that same cruise. They planned to travel with another couple with whom they were good friends. At the last minute Bill decided to cancel the trip and spend the money instead on a small power boat and bought the 21-foot cabin cruiser. Their friends followed through with their plans and took the trip. They died in the accident. I asked them if they knew where their friends had been sitting. Mary didn't know but as I noticed that Mary was a smoker I asked if their friends were smokers as well. Mary replied that they both smoked. I explained that all of the smokers were seated in the back of the plane. That was a question on the form from Royal Cruise Line who assigned the seats to the passengers. Bill realized that they would have been sitting with them, and as I explained, none of those passengers survived. From then on we were good friends.

As I developed confidence in operating my boat I took her out more often. Because I worked swing shift in those days most mornings during the week I went to the marina and played on my boat. I met more of my neighbors on the dock and continued to take short cruises out the long channel, Redwood Creek, to San Francisco Bay. On the weekends, I would head north on the west side of the bay, passing under the San Mateo bridge, on to the waterfront of San Francisco. It was a delight to see the Ferry Building and Coit Tower, great landmarks of the City by the Bay. I could make the round trip in three hours at a cruising speed of about 20 knots. At that speed the engine burned seven gallons of gas per hour. In 1977 the price of gas was 50 cents per gallon. Three years later that price had tripled.

I decided to add some more accessories to the boat. The biggest of these was fresh water cooling. That would eliminate salt water from circulating through the engine block. Fresh water would circulate through a heat exchanger to cool the engine. While the boat was out of the water at the dealership I made arrangements to have the boat's name painted on the stern.

Grand Canary became a frequent visitor to the open bay and the fuel dock at the neighboring marina, Pete's Harbor. I took some new friends with me but also friends from work and home. My neighbor lady, Odarka, who had hosted the potluck upon my return from Tenerife, and a friend of hers, came with me one afternoon. My parents and siblings came for a visit as well.

Docking was the only operational part of boating that made me nervous. The boat did not steer well at low speed and it took quite a while to gain my confidence in that maneuver. Docking in the slip was like parking a car in a parking space. The main dock was in front of me and there were two short docks on both sides known as fingers. Once I got the boat's bow between the fingers I was alright. Docking at the fuel dock was much easier. That was a long straight dock and all I had to do was pull up parallel to it and tie up to the cleats. With experience I became good at both maneuvers.

Boating became a big part of my life. I enjoyed being out on the water. At times on the return leg of a cruise I would pull the throttles back to a fast idle. I would move slowly across the water, just enjoying all the senses of sight and smell of the bay. I just liked being out there, on the water.

As the summer of 1977 turned into fall I was still busy visiting doctors and my attorney. My attorney decided early on that my case did not warrant a jury trial and we would settle out of court. He was in touch with other attorneys who were representing clients in this case. I understood most of the legal aspects of the case and was interested in the legal technicalities so Jerry made the effort to explain the details of what was going on. We were getting close to final negotiations when my back pain suddenly got worse. I think I lifted something that wasn't that heavy but was more than ten pounds. Jerry explained that we could not settle the case when my physical status was still changing. So I went back to the neurologist who was handling my care. The neurologist was not satisfied with my recovery performance and referred me to an orthopedist. My new doctor told me to stop wearing the brace around my lower waist and perform some special leg lift floor exercises to strengthen my lower back. Soon I was back on the road to recovery, or what passed for recovery.

It soon became clear that my back would never be the same as it was before the jump off the wing of the burning 747. I began to adjust to the "new normal" of my life. My weight lifting capacity would be limited to ten pounds. Once I accepted that, I concentrated even harder on the exercises every day. I made a big improvement in my emotional distress as well.

One night in bed I dreamt about Hans Hofman, the fat Dutchman who stole my film. He was cutting a hole in the side of the wall and crawling into my bedroom. I rolled over, grabbed a revolver and shot the intruder dead. He never came back after that.

❧ Chapter 14 ❦

FLYING RECOVERY

In October, 1977, I felt that I was ready to fly again. The idea of traveling has always appealed to me. During my freshman year of high school I took a geography course. I was interested in where land masses were, what the weather and the people were like, and the history of people who lived there. We in the United States were led to believe that we Americans were the best people in the world, we should be the leaders and everyone should look up to us. I was a little doubtful about that. Some civilizations had been in existence since way before Europeans landed in North America. I wanted to see what it was like "over there" and the fastest way to get there was to fly.

Getting back on a jetliner became a priority for me. With my travel agent's assistance, I booked a flight to San Diego. I planned to fly down on a Saturday and back in the same day, leaving from San Francisco. When the day came I found that I was not quite as brave as I thought I was.

As I made my way from the ticket counter to the gate area I became pretty nervous. There were no security check points as we know them now but airline personnel were checking tickets, I think. Everyone I saw there seemed to be normal but I wasn't. As aircraft arrived at gates and passengers deplaned, I began to get a feeling of how ordinary this form of transportation had become. There was an inherent risk in commercial aviation but it was minimal. I was an example of what could go wrong. But I was confident enough in the aviation system that I was ready to fly again. From my seat, as the door of the plane closed, I had to fight the urge to get up and run off the plane! As we taxied for takeoff, I could see out the window that the sky was clear and fog was not a problem. I read a lot about the technical aspects of flight. I could see that the flaps on the trailing edge of the wing and the slats on the leading edge were extended. That gave more lift to the plane. I understood the conversation that was taking place between the tower and the cockpit.

Then we were number one for takeoff. That was my favorite part of a flight. The feeling of the power of the jet engines pushing that big aluminum tube down the runway was exciting to me. I could get an impression of speed as we made our way down the runway. As we got to takeoff speed I could feel the nose wheel rise and the ground began to fall away. Then the sound of the landing gear rising into the aircraft gave way to the sound of the jet engines pushing us higher in the air until we leveled off at our assigned altitude.

The flight attendants started the in-flight beverage service. I noticed how young they were. I had just turned 30 and was very happy about it. After all, I almost didn't make it that far. I was shaking, trying not to think too much about smoke and flames inside a jetliner.

The fear was starting to subside when the flight attendant reached my row. As she asked me what I would like to drink, my mouth seemed to open but no words came out. She asked me again and I got the word seven out. She asked me if I wanted Seven and Seven and I shook my head no. She asked me again if I wanted 7Up and I nodded yes. As the flight attendant handed me the drink, I was shaking so much that I almost spilled the whole thing. Somehow I got it to my tray and left it there for a while. I almost spilled it again when I took a sip. Thankfully, our descent into San Diego was about to start and my glass was picked up.

As we got closer to landing I could see high rise buildings just outside the window. We were lower than the top floor and I could see people inside. I was hoping that we would miss the structures and land safely. Then I saw the perimeter fence and the captain was standing on the brakes. It was a hard stop almost like the one in Tenerife.

We made a turn to the left and I looked out the window to see if another plane was coming at us. I could imagine that smoke filled the aircraft. But there was no smoke. Our plane was at the end of the runway. There was no room for another plane. We made our way to the gate and stopped. The other passengers seemed nonchalant about their arrival in San Diego but I realized that we had cheated death again. I was in a hurry to get off the plane. I found the men's room right away and lost my breakfast. As I cleaned up, I felt much better and made my way out to the curb.

I asked a skycap what bus I should take to get to the famous San Diego Zoo. He explained the number to take to downtown, then how to change to another bus with a transfer to the zoo. I got inside the zoo and rode a skyway tram for an overview of the big park. Then I spent the rest of the afternoon walking around the many exhibits until late in the afternoon. I had an 8 pm return flight to SFO and was at the gate in plenty of time.

My seatmate on the return flight was a young mother with a small child. I was very comfortable being on the plane with them. This was almost like a renewal of life. I was delighted to see this little child crawling around her mother's lap, looking at all the things around her. Life goes on and I am glad to be a part of it. I was in an aisle seat this time so I could not see out the window very well. The captain pushed the throttle up and we jumped into the air. Soon we were over the ocean and headed north. I had no fear now. If a mother and her baby could be on this flight, so could I. We flew low on final approach to SFO and I could see the bay. I looked for boats and marinas. I had a new relationship with the bay now and I really liked it.

In early November 1977, I went on another flight. I wanted to know that I was mostly recovered from a fear of flying. This second flight was also a one day event, on a Saturday. The plan was to fly south from San Francisco (SFO) to Los Angeles (LAX), turn around and fly back. This simple flight plan turned out to be a test of courage. I felt very confident as I made my way to the gate for our departure to LAX. After boarding and taking our seats the flight attendants went through their routine safety instructions. Even before they said so, I counted the rows in front of me as well as behind me to the nearest exit door. I knew where I would go if I had to get off this plane in a hurry. As we waited for our turn for takeoff, the captain announced that we were ready and asked the flight attendants to take their seats. I was really paying attention to what was going on. I heard the engines throttle up, then they came back to idle again. I was on full alert! Something is wrong! The engine throttled up again but came back to idle right away. The captain came on the intercom and said that there was a problem with the plane. We would go back to the gate and board another plane that was about to arrive from Boise. I think my seatmates could hear my heart pounding!

All of the passengers were asked to gather at the next gate for our delayed departure to LAX. The three flight crew members were standing near the main aisle, chatting. I walked over to them and began a conversation. I explained that this was my second practice flight and I was doing OK. I held up my hands to show that I was not shaking too bad. They asked what do you mean and I explained that I was a survivor of the accident in Tenerife. Their eyes got very big! They explained that one of the landing gear lights was not working properly and they were not going to take any chances. It probably was just a faulty light bulb but they didn't want to find out the hard way. I felt comfortable with their decision and was ready to try it again.

We boarded a new plane and made our way out to one of the main runways for takeoff. San Francisco International Airport has two sets of runways at right angles to each other. As we taxied on to an active runway for takeoff, I could look out the right window and see aircraft on final approach. That was not a problem in clear weather. In fog or rain the air traffic controllers could only use one set of runways. With precision, the engines spooled up and increased thrust, which propelled us down the runway. I like to guess when the nose wheel rises off the asphalt, called rotation. I was pretty close again as we climbed out over San Francisco Bay. I was at ease as the flight attendants began the beverage service. I could easily ask for my favorite beverage, 7Up or Sprite, and drink it without spilling a drop.

Our descent into the Los Angeles basin was interesting as I watched all the houses and buildings disappear under us. I didn't even think about my flight into LAX that previous March on my first leg to the Canary Islands. We landed smoothly and taxied to the gate. During that time the flight attendants gave out flight information about departing flights. We were almost an hour late arriving at LAX so some passengers had to really scramble to get to their next flight. I wasn't worried as I had at least another half hour to wait for my return flight to SFO.

My departing flight from LAX was ready for boarding at a nearby gate when I arrived. I got in line and made my way to my seat. I wasn't nervous at all as I waited for the rest of the passengers to board. About the time the door closed, the captain's voice came on the intercom. There was a problem with the navigation system. The gyro compass was not working properly and a replacement was on its way. After about ten minutes the captain spoke to us again. He explained that it would take too long to repair the compass so we needed to change planes. We were on United and I think we got on PSA. The captain explained that PSA was at the next gate and they had room for all the passengers. The ground crew would move our baggage for us and we would be about 15 minutes late leaving LAX. A message would be sent to our former arrival gate at SFO so that anyone who was meeting our flight could find us.

This was just incredible! What were the odds of being forced to change planes on BOTH ends of a fight? I had already beaten the astronomical odds in the accident in Tenerife. I was part of 10% of the passengers who had survived the worst aircraft accident in world history. Out of 618 people on both planes I was among 74 of the initial survivors and in a subgroup of 14 walking survivors. I felt that the flight to LA was a test. God was testing me. And I was ready! We took off from LAX and landed at SFO without further incident. What an amazing day that was! My co-workers were surprised as well when I told them the story.

By 1978 I felt that I was ready for the next big step in my road to recovery. I decided to take the same cruise over again. I still wanted to see all those ports of call around the Mediterranean Sea where the Golden Odyssey would dock. From the Rock of Gibraltar to the big rock formation of the port of Valetta in Malta and the stone pillars of the Acropolis in Athens, my imagination raced ahead. My attorney explained that the settlement would include the refund for the cruise. A separate refund was what I had in mind but that was not to be. I contacted co-survivor Jim Naik of Royal Cruise Lines in San Francisco and made arrangements to go on the same cruise that I started in 1977. It was then that I asked Jim to get me the same seat on the Pan Am flight that I had before. I wanted to sit in 30C again. No problem, he said.

My case with the airlines was proceeding well by January of 1978. I had no further back problems as long as I did not lift anything over 10 pounds. I continued doing the stretch and leg lift exercises as outlined by my medical doctor. The written report from the psychiatrist was not all that great from a legal point of view but it was okay. The cuts in my eyes had healed by late summer 1977. Physically and mentally I was progressing well.

There were four defendants in the civil case that surrounded the aircraft accident in Tenerife. They were KLM, Pan Am, the government of Spain (as they owned the airport) and Boeing, the manufacturers of the 747s. The defendants decided which party was most to blame for the accident and assigned a percentage of the damages to each party. They contracted with a brokerage firm in New York, United States Aviation Underwriters Inc., to handle all of the negotiations out of court. After further negotiations with USAU we settled my case for an undisclosed amount.

I was pleased with the final results and was ready to get on with my life. I paid off the loan on the boat, traded my spinet for a theatre console organ, paid for the repeat trip and had money left over for emergencies. Life was good!

~ Chapter 15 ~

REACHING THE GOLDEN
ODYSSEY, FINALLY

The last Saturday in March of 1978 was like a TV rerun. It all seemed rather familiar. I took a cab from Palo Alto to SFO this time. I don't remember the flight to LAX but I felt a little strange at the gate there. There was no need to disturb anyone by sharing that I had been on this trip the year before. I believe Royal Cruise Lines had a representative there who accompanied us to the ship, but I don't recall. The Pan Am 747 was at the gate and we boarded on time. This aircraft was also part of the airlines charter fleet so seat 30C was in the same location as before. Another couple was sitting next to me again with the wife by the window just as the year before. We exchanged pleasantries and then we were off to JFK in New York to change crew, refuel and board a few more passengers. We had an eleven hour flight ahead of us. I managed to catnap a little on that leg of the flight.

About an hour before our arrival in Las Palmas, Canary Islands I got a little nervous. Would we divert again or not? When the captain spoke on the intercom my heart rate doubled, or so it seemed. The captain told us that we would be landing in Las Palmas on time. Most of us had been awake for a few hours by then. The slight nervousness I felt before vanished with his announcement. Soon we could see a bit of land in the distance. The huge and graceful 747 descended through some light puffy clouds and the island of Grand Canary became visible to us. We landed smoothly and taxied to our designated spot on the tarmac. The terminal did not have jetways so we deplaned down a stairway at the left front door to a waiting bus which took us to the terminal. We didn't have to go through customs and immigration because we were heading straight to the ship and departing the port. After we went upstairs to the main floor, we continued outside to a waiting bus for the ride to the ship.

As I entered the terminal I got quite a surprise! Several men in suits were standing by the wall as we walked by. One of them was not wearing a suit and we immediately recognized each other. He was Juan Antonio Munillo Rivas, the

Pan Am ground crew chief. He was one of two men who came on board Clipper Victor on Tenerife through the nose wheel access hatch and made their way to the cockpit. He was also a survivor! I dashed over and shook hands with him. What a big surprise that was! Then one of the men in a suit, whom I presumed was a cruise line employee, told me that I should rejoin the group and get on the bus to the ship. Soon the bus was heading out of the airport to the harbor where Golden Odyssey waited for us.

We boarded the Golden Odyssey via a narrow gangway through a doorway on a lower deck. A line of ship's mates stood there waiting for us. They looked at my paperwork and one of them took me to my assigned cabin. It was all very efficient. With all of us aboard, the crew cast off the dock lines and we made our way out to sea.

The first item of business for all passengers was a safety drill. If you have been on a cruise, you know what it's like. I got my lifejacket from its hook inside my cabin door, put it on and headed for my assigned life boat station, which was noted on the inside door of my cabin. As I arrived at my assigned lifeboat station, we had just cleared the breakwater surrounding the harbor and I quickly realized that this was not San Francisco Bay. There was a little bit of wind but the waves were 18 to 20 feet high! As the 10,000 ton ship lurched over each wave, a few passengers were getting a little green or pale. Roll call by cabin number was quickly accomplished and we were dismissed. Several people got sick on the way back to their cabins. I made it to mine but just barely. Being a boater I was somewhat used to a rolling vessel but not like this. We were mostly going up and down over the waves but there was a little side to side motion as well. Not many people ate dinner that night.

By morning we had arrived in Funchal, Madeira. The main shore excursion there was a bus ride to the top of a mountain, then a ride down the hill in a sled that traveled on a smooth path made of leaves. That was different. Madeira is a Portuguese possession whereas the Canary Islands are part of Spain. I won't bore you with details of each port of call on this cruise. However, some of them stick out in my mind.

Gibraltar is famous as the gateway to the Mediterranean. The south side of this relatively narrow body of water is Tangier, Morocco. The two cities are very different. Tangier is built on low rising hills and is very Arabic. Instead of a tour I walked from the port into the city center. Along the way several young men approached me looking for money. They were starting to hassle me when a couple from the ship approached and called out to me. The young men dispersed and I continued to walk with my shipmates. I was glad they had appeared. This was not like walking in your own neighborhood.

Gibraltar is a city state built on a huge rock overlooking the Mediterranean. We had an interesting docking maneuver there. As a power boat owner I was interested in watching the docking process. The wind was blowing pretty hard towards the dock. To avoid slamming his ship into the dock the captain ordered the crew to drop the anchor when the ship was about 50 feet from the stone pier. With the ship stabilized by the anchor the captain ordered the anchor chain to be released slowly. That allowed the ship to arrive at the dock very slowly which avoided damage to the ship. I was quite impressed! The city center is right next to the port. I walked around through the rows and rows of high end duty free shops. I didn't see anything that I wanted so I headed back to the ship.

The next port was Majorca, a large Spanish island southwest of Spain. I took the city tour there. The part I liked best was the beach area. It was wide with white sand and the blue Mediterranean lapping at its shore. Okay, maybe the best part was seeing the ladies on the beach. As is the custom in Europe, most of the ladies were topless.

One nice thing about this cruise is that I could see many different civilizations. If I see a place I like, I might be inclined to go back there at another time. I would like to see Majorca again but I haven't made it back there yet.

On one of the days when we were out to sea all day, I was walking around the ship when I saw my seatmates from the flight from LAX. We were in an interior stairway when we stopped and chatted a while. They asked me how I liked the cruise so far and I replied that it was better than last year. The man dropped his head as he readily understood that I was a survivor of the aircraft accident in Tenerife.

He then explained that he is a lawyer in Los Angeles and represented the plaintiffs in federal court. He was the lead attorney who was trying to get the trials to be held in Los Angeles. His team lost and the plaintiffs, including Pan Am, won the right to move all of the civil trials to New York City, Pan Am's headquarters. He asked where I was sitting at the time of the accident and I explained that I was in the same seat that I had this trip. A co-survivor with the cruise line arranged for me to get the same seat, 30C, per my request. Then I explained that the couple who were sitting in their seats last year, 30A and 30B, were crushed on impact. All three of us were quite shaken by these revelations. Talk about a small world.

I am interested in World War II history and the port of Valletta, Malta, offered some insights into that era. The port itself is made or cut out of stone. Instead of a breakwater that surrounds a port or marina at a height of fifteen feet above sea level, the walls in the port of Valletta are 50 feet high. Malta was founded by the Knights of Saint Johns of Jerusalem. The order left the Holy Lands after the failure of the Crusades, creating settlements in Rhodes and Malta. The natural fortification of the island of Malta protected the knights from the marauding Muslims. Most of the island is made of stone. The solid rock was carved to provide living space for people and protection of the port. The underground caverns provided safety to the people of Malta when they were pummeled from the air by German bombers during World War II. The Nazis dropped lots and lots of bombs on Malta in an attempt to take control of the island. Had they been successful they would have had the ability to control the flow of ship and air traffic between Italy and North Africa. The Nazi Luftwaffe was unable to achieve their goal to control Malta. However, very few people died on Malta because the stone island provided safety for them. The port of Valletta is also home to an impressive cathedral, which was built on a large open area. I saw several of these structures later in life on travels through Europe.

Another interesting place we visited was the island of Crete in the eastern Mediterranean. Crete was the home of the Minoan civilization. They became a seafaring nation, by necessity, and traded goods with neighbors in Egypt to the south and Greece to the north. Our ship docked in the port city of Heraklion and we visited the ruins of a village in Knossos. Standing on a walkway we could see the remains of large ceramic pots that once held food. Not long after this trip National Geographic Magazine published an article about this island and posted a photo from the same location. It has always been a cool thing for me to see photos of places I have visited. In my mind I can visualize what is just outside the photo's field of view.

The ancient people of Crete were known for their architecture. They created stone columns that were bigger on the top than on the bottom, the opposite of the Greek design. We saw several examples of this in Knossos. The entire civilization on Crete was destroyed by a giant wall of water that was created when the volcanic island of Santorini exploded, about 3,600 years ago. Santorini is a small island to the north of Crete. The volcano that created the island had a stone cap over the top of it. That stone cap held in the pressure that came from deep underground. The pressure built up to the point where the stone cover gave way in a massive explosion. The resulting wave has been estimated to have been 200 feet high. It washed over Crete and destroyed almost everything and everybody.

Santorini was our next to last stop. We didn't actually stop there. Several openings in the side of the caldera provide access to ships so they can sail in one side and out the other. Our ship performed a 360 degree turn at the base of the largest cliff in the middle of the old volcano's caldera. The caldera itself is probably ten to twelve miles across. On its eastern side is a cliff about 300 feet high. On top of the cliff is a small town with houses built of cement and painted white as is common in Greece. To get to the town, there is a footpath to the top. A person can walk up the path or ride in a donkey with a local guide. After the Golden Odyssey made the 360 degree rotation, we continued north out of the volcano to our last stop, Piraeus, the port of Athens.

We had one day to visit the famous city of Athens. After our arrival in early morning, we were ushered off the ship to an awaiting bus. I chose to take a tour of the Acropolis, a huge site with many buildings. Our tour bus took us to the base of a hill and we walked to the top of a nice plateau in the heart of Athens. There before us was the huge famous building, the Parthenon, completed in 438 BC. Seeing it on TV or in a movie is one thing but seeing it in person is quite another. Setting a column upright is an engineering marvel but how did the ancient Greeks get the huge blocks of marble on TOP of those columns? It was all quite amazing.

After the tour of the Parthenon we were delivered to a hotel. We were not given rooms there but we had access to the public areas while we spent the rest of the day waiting for our long flight to LAX. I joined several other travelers and went to a movie in a nearby theatre. I recall that it was about the Swedish musical group ABBA. I liked their music so it was a pleasant way to spend the afternoon. Back at the hotel some of my new friends told me that another couple, among the passengers, were also survivors of the Tenerife accident. I tried to find them but was unsuccessful. We felt that the cruise line put us on a different seating schedule (I was in the first seating) so that we would not meet and discuss the accident with other passengers. I have no idea who they were. But I was glad that they were healthy enough to travel, just as I was.

Our departure from Athens was about two hours late. We had to get off the ship by 8 am the morning of the ship's arrival in Athens and were up all day with no ability to take a nap. So everybody was tired when we boarded the Pan Am 747 at 2 am on Saturday bound for LAX. We had a fuel stop in Brussels, then continued to JFK in New York. All of the passengers had to deplane there to go through customs and immigration. The West Coast passengers reboarded the same plane and continued to LAX. After retrieving my bag, I boarded another plane for the one hour flight to SFO. By the time I got home to Palo Alto, I had been up for 32 hours. I slept pretty well that night! I had finally completed the trip I had started the year before.

I had been feeling apprehensive during the last hour of the flight from New York to Las Palmas. I felt confident about the flight crew on this flight, and all Pan Am flights. I worked through my PTSD through therapy with Dr. Rawson and I developed new confidence in the aviation service industry by flying those two short trips within California. My confidence in the industry was partly a matter of mind over matter.

It wasn't easy but I accomplished my goal. I wanted to travel outside of the United States to see places that I had read about. I wanted to satisfy my need to find out what it was like "over there". I rationalized my fear with the data on airline safety. The likelihood of dying in a commercial airline accident was about one in a million, that is, from a statistical point of view, a person would have to fly a million times to have one chance of being in an fatal accident. And even then, the chances of survival of that accident are pretty good.

They are even better now.

LIFE GOES ON

A month before I departed on the repeat cruise through the Mediterranean I changed jobs. Teledyne MEC had been my home for nine years but I felt that it was time to move on. I felt that I had reached my peak achievement there. I accepted an offer from Hewlett-Packard at a division in Palo Alto, with an understanding that I would be on unpaid leave for two weeks to go on the repeat cruise.

HP made test equipment at that time and I was chosen to work as a technician on passive microwave devices. For most of the time I tuned and tested coaxial directional couplers. Those devices are used in microwave test systems to monitor the power level in the system. The building complex where I worked was right across the back parking lot of Teledyne MEC, all of which was in the Stanford Industrial Park in Palo Alto.

Dave Packard and Bill Hewlett were electrical engineering graduates of Stanford University in Palo Alto and started their company in Bill's garage on Addison Avenue in Palo Alto in the late 1930s. Their first product was an audio oscillator, which emitted sound at a variable, tunable frequency. One of their first customers was the Walt Disney Company, which used that product in the production of the animated feature film *Fantasia*. The microwave test equipment product line soon followed.

After about a year or two at HP I lost contact with friends at Teledyne MEC. But I did hear that the company moved from Palo Alto to the Sacramento area in 1984. At times I wondered what my life would have been like had I stayed with them. Life is full of choices. Sometimes choices are forced on us when a door closes. Sometimes we make our own choices. When one door closes, another door opens.

My division of HP moved from Palo Alto to Santa Rosa in 1991. HP had divisions there and in the neighboring town of Rohnert Park, an hour's drive north of San Francisco. I was chosen to go with the division's move and was glad for the change in scenery. Instead of another mobile home I was able to buy a condominium instead. That move worked out very well for me.

I met a neighbor lady in the condo complex in Santa Rosa named Paula. She was also a resident owner and we began dating in 1992. The relationship with Paula lasted about five years. She enjoyed sailing with me on my Catalina 27 sailboat, KIYOTEE, which I bought new in 1981, after I sold the Reinell 247B power boat. (I moved the boat from Redwood City to Ballena Isle Marina in Alameda, next to Oakland, in 1984) She also liked to travel so we went on a cruise through the Caribbean and spent a week in Hawaii. Prior to moving to Santa Rosa I could live cheaply in my mobile home and travel. Owning the condo slowed down my travel plans but I was still able to travel once a year.

ॐ Chapter 17 ॐ

FINDING THE FAT DUTCHMAN, HANS HOFMAN

A fter the repeat cruise in 1978, I went to London and Amsterdam in May of 1979. I spent a week in each city, starting with London. I traveled from London to Amsterdam by train. The hotel where I had a reservation was quite a distance from the downtown area. But I rode public transit and brought a good map of Amsterdam with me from California.

The editor of the Dutch magazine *Niewe Review* had provided me with the address of Hans Hofman, the man I call the Fat Dutchman who stole my film from the Hotel Mencey shop in Santa Cruz de Tenerife. Using my map, on my second day in Amsterdam, I was able to locate his address of Amstel 4, which is just off the main street of Damrak. Next door was a small coffee shop. I inquired about Hans Hofman there. They knew him and knew about my photos as well. That evening, as I waited around nearby, Hans drove up. We immediately recognized each other. As I walked up to his car, he rolled the passenger window down and said, "Hello, David Wiley." He invited me to get in to his car and we drove around the neighborhood. He heard that an American was looking for him.

His story was that the *Niewe Review* editor had sold the photos around Europe, which I knew was a lie. The photo editor at the *Sunday Times* of London told my attorney that Hans Hofman himself brought copies of my photos to the newspaper building. He demanded cash and was paid by check. After Hans left the newspaper office, the photo editor contacted their attorney who realized the photos were stolen. They jumped in a car and raced to the bank to cancel the check but Hans had already cashed it and left. The editor then contacted Pan Am who verified my name. The editor chose to publish one photo anyway with my name on it. We settled out of court later for a small undisclosed amount. They would not tell us how much they paid Hans Hofman. My guess is that Hans got between $30,000 and $45,000 from each publication including *Stern* from Germany (West

Germany at that time) and *Paris Match* from France. We did not approach the other publications.

Hans Hofman arranged to interview me at my hotel in Amsterdam. After that we drove out to the airport so he could take a photo of me there with aircraft in the background. The interview was published in another small Dutch magazine *RITS*. (That one included a photograph that I had heard about, a photo of me standing beside the runway on Tenerife. I am reaching into my right rear pocket to retrieve my handkerchief to wipe blood off the right side of my head. My camera is clearly visible hanging around my neck.)

He also told me that he would get copies of my photos to me on Friday. He knew I was leaving town on Saturday and he never delivered the copies. I was so close but so far away from recovering my property. I was disappointed but I knew that he knew that somebody was after him.

∞   Chapter 18   ∞

WHERE IS THE GOLDEN ODYSSEY TODAY?

I have wondered what happened to the cruise ship Golden Odyssey. It was pretty easy to find out. While online, I typed the ship's name into my favorite search engine. I readily found photos and information about the ship. She was sold by Royal Cruise Line and is currently at anchor in Hong Kong harbor. She was renamed Macau Success and is used as a gambling ship on overnight cruises.

Here are the details about the Golden Odyssey. Built in 1974 for Royal Cruise Lines, Piraeus, at Helsingar Vaerft, Denmark. RCL sold in 1989 to Kloster cruise, Nassau. Sold 1994 to Deutsche Seetouristik, Nassau, renamed ASTRA II, chartered to Caravelle Shipping, cruising for Neckermann Seereisen. Laid-up Genoa 1997 after the end of Caravelle charter. Chartered to Hapag-Lloyd Kreuzfarten, 1998. Sold in 2001 following end of Hapag-Lloyd charter to Asia Cruise Club, Nassau; renamed OMAR II for overnight gambling cruises from Hong Kong. Transferred to Success Cruises in 2004 and renamed MACAU SUCCESS; presently (2005) in service on overnight cruises from Macau.

BIBLIOGRAPHY

Aviation Week and Space Technology – Spaniards Analyze Tenerife Accident – November 20, 1978, 113-121

Aviation Week and Space Technology – Clearances Cited in Tenerife Accident – November 27, 1978, 67–73

"Terror At Tenerife" – Norman Williams, 149–151,1977 by Bible Voice, Van Nuys, California

Wikipedia – PSA Flight 182 – 2/26/11

ALPA.org

Cruise Critic Message Boards – Royal Cruise Lines Fleet History

 ~ Chapter 19 ~

HOW THE ACCIDENT CHANGED
MY SIBLINGS' LIVES

A major trauma like the Tenerife plane crash affects not just the survivor but all of his/her friends and family members as well. While I was writing this book, my editor, Diane Nelson Abel, suggested I ask each of my siblings to talk with me a bit about their memories of the time of the accident and how/if this has changed their lives in any way.

My sister Marcia was married and living in Missoula, Montana in 1977. Here's what she had to say: "I was living in Missoula, Montana, house sitting for a professor of art while he and his wife were on sabbatical leave for six months. My husband, Rick Cliff, was finishing a Master of Fine Arts degree at the University of Montana. I was working for a dentist as a dental assistant, as a bridge to a career as either a hygienist or dentist.

"Then the phone call came. It was Mom, telling me that David, my older brother, had been in a plane crash. Our sister, Cheryl, had been listening to the radio, when it was announced that there had been a horrific plane crash of two 747s in Tenerife in the Canary Islands. 'Isn't that the plane David is on,' she asked? And the answer was an ominous yes.

"That evening and for days we watched television news coverage. I looked and looked at the debris, searching for anything familiar of my brother's.

"I was so thankful that he was alive. I remember asking if he was burned. I was again thankful that he was not.

"And I cried when David was able to call us, to tell us in person that he was among the few walking injured.

"The crash affected more than only those on the plane. A patient told about being in Central America, and how the crash dominated the news for three weeks. Rick and I separated after his graduation and I started pre-dental studies at the U of Montana. One of my floormates talked about the world's worst aviation disaster.

Her aunt was on that plane, too, seated toward the back and did not survive. Years later, the father of our daughter's husband, a 747 pilot for Eastern Airlines, told of flying over Tenerife shortly after the crash and commenting that that is where the accident was. Right down there.

"There have been many changes in my life since the crash: Divorce from my first husband, three years of pre-dental studies, four years of dental school, starting a dental practice in my hometown, marriage to my classmate, Corey Stanley, our first real house, our first baby, Emily, our second house, our second baby, Tyler, selling our very successful 15 year-old practice due to my heart problems related to stress and Corey joining the Air Force as a dentist, uprooting the kids and moving to our first base in Okinawa, Japan, Corey's residency in Periodontics in San Antonio, Texas, graduations of our children from high school then colleges, marriages of each of them, and promotions for my husband.

"There was one change I hadn't counted on or realized was happening.

"During dental school and the early days of the practice, we had little money and so did not fly much. But as we became more successful, it seemed easier to just hop on a plane and fly to conventions, reunions, vacations, wherever we needed to go rather than tiring ourselves by driving. I began to notice a strange change in me. I'd have my husband and the kids, in grade school now, hold my hands when we took off. Their reward was a TicTac. I thought it was strange, when I opened my eyes one time, to see Tyler enjoying looking out the window at the other planes and the scenery. I thought, doesn't he realize how dangerous this can be? Most airplane accidents happen on take-off or landing. Had I not told him the story of his uncle who was almost killed in an airplane accident?

"Then the day came when I had to fly by myself. I couldn't very well ask my seatmate to hold my hand! Nope! I had to be an adult. I reflected on the world's worst aviation disaster and the fear and panic David must have felt. And I found myself praying. Praying to God as I often have done. Telling Him that I am Your child. My life is in Your hands. Always has been, and forever will be. Whatever your plans are for me, I know that I am with You and You are with me.

"My faith has been incredibly increased. Not that I don't check to see where the nearest exit is on the plane, because I do. Yes, I even look behind me, just as the flight attendants tell us to do. But I know, with never a doubt, that I am in God's hands. He has blessed me over and over again and not just on airplanes, but in relationships, career choices, schools, tests, traffic, and every endeavor I can remember, starting well before the plane crash. And I'm not afraid to tell of my faith, what the Lord has done in my life and to publicly say thank you to Him.

"Someone has said that there is no great loss without some small gain. And this is my change, my gain: One step of many on the path to a deeper and unshakable faith in God and the courage to say thank you to Him."

My brother Dan, ten years younger than I, talks about his reactions this way:

"I started my flying time at the age of 12 and became interested in all types of aircraft. Amazed at the size and weight of a 747, the power that makes it fly, the wings that hold it up, landing gear that lets it roll, the lucky people who get to operate and fly a 747. When I had heard of the accident in the Canary Islands, I was stunned that someone, "the pilot", had screwed up so badly as to destroy not only one 747 but two 747s. Later realizing that my brother was on that flight brought fear, shock, and the thought of not knowing. Wondering if David was alive or burnt alive! Parents were freaking out. Dad was physically shaking and at times not able to speak. Mom wandered around the kitchen keeping herself busy. For me, I didn't get that cold chill that goes down your back. That feeling my brother was gone. I had felt that feeling before and knew the feeling well. But it wasn't there. Scared I may be wrong, it took another nine hours before we saw on the news David Wiley on the list.

"For me the whole thing, once again, made me realize that life is too short. Do not take the time a person has on this earth without a whole lot of laughter, a spot of fun, a smile on your face. When it is time, and only God knows when it is time, for you to go. A person will not cheat death. I have lived my life with a smile on my face and not worried about things I cannot do anything about. Things like this bring it all back to me as a time of remembrance. What is important. What is not.

"Dave on the other hand was shaken and stirred. Fiberglass landed in his eyes and cut the surface, making his eyes freeze up at night and hard to open in the mornings. When we were alone he talked of the smells, the people running, the sounds. Like the sounds of people screaming, the relief when the front section broke off the back half and people ran out. Escaping certain doom. In the fog not knowing what had taken place, the fog lifted only to see the rest of the disaster. To be one of fourteen people that could walk!

"Yes, David was shaken and stirred! He finally found a thrill, something that makes him smile, something to look forward to, sailing! It took years to get that scared look out of his face. You know, the look of being so scared and traumatized. It was in his eyes for so long. That's where you see it. The brain has a capacity to filter the bad stuff and keep the good. David will never forget, he can't. But the bad of the bad has escaped him, thank God! It's a hell of a thing to live with, but David will be just fine."

My youngest sibling, my sister Cheryl, wrote the following to me:

"I have delayed writing this because I'm not sure what to say. We have lived with it for so long and I was young.

"What I have seen in you:

"I have seen that this terrible accident has proven to me that you are a Survivor. You were able to think quick on your feet and help people to safety. You were not selfish at all to only think of yourself. Somehow you had the instinct to take pictures during this horrific event. Wow! What a treasure. I have seen that you persevere in whatever you choose. You have been thrown some curve balls, like losing your job, but were still able to come out of that okay. I know that this was a terrible experience and it has haunted you for a long time. I am glad that you are able to embrace what happened and go forward instead of having it hold you back.

"I see that sailing is your solace. Nothing bad can hurt you or maybe it is your meditation time. Whatever, I see your passion with it and appreciate the fact that you were able to find something you like to do instead of sitting on the couch and worrying about what could have been."

"I am glad to be the sister of a Survivor. I am proud to say that my brother was one of the fourteen walking survivors of this horrific crash. I feel as if I was part of history too even though I saw it from a different perspective. My faith in God was renewed and I am reminded of it every time I think of the crash. I feel that God protected David from dying and showed him the hole in the ceiling to crawl out of. Yes, he was hurt but not dead. Somehow the strength in David came from within through Him. I look at David and see his passion for life and his kindness. I try to have the strength that he has to carry on. I have embraced the accident but it doesn't consume me totally. I am glad that I am a Survivor too. When David survived the accident, we all (our family) became survivors. I am glad to spend each moment with my family because you never know when it may be taken away."

≈ Chapter 20 ≈

I CHOOSE NOT TO LIVE IN FEAR: BUILDING A HAPPY LIFE FOR MYSELF

In 1984 I moved my sailboat, a Catalina 27 named "KIYOTEE," from Redwood City to Alameda. In 2000 I sold "KIYOTEE" and bought a used Catalina 30 sailboat, which I renamed "JAMAICA 3." This one is named for my favorite destination and is my third boat. Both sailboats were made by the same company in southern California.

Ballena Isle Marina is my home away from home on the weekends now. Alameda is bordered by Oakland and is across the bay from San Francisco and is south of the San Francisco-Oakland Bay Bridge. The marina is a one hour and ten minute drive south of my home in Santa Rosa. I am on the boat every weekend and I enjoy being out on the water. If it's too windy, I stay in port and I don't sail in the rain. Otherwise I am on the bay enjoying the sun, wind and water.

I am also very active in the Ballena Bay Yacht Club. Most non-boaters think yacht clubs are for rich, snooty people. That is not the case with most clubs. Most boaters give up other things in life to have a boat. The yacht club is a social outlet and is a great way to meet other boaters in the marina. One does not even have to own a boat to belong to the yacht club and several members fall into that category. We have our own bar and most Saturday nights one of our members hosts a dinner. After dinner we fire up the juke box and dance the night away. Other members like to sit around and have discussions about topical subjects. It's a laid back atmosphere. I spend Saturday nights on the boat and sail again on Sunday before driving back to Santa Rosa. Now that I am partly retired I sometimes spend three or four day weekends on the boat. It's a great lifestyle!

Around three or four years ago, probably in 2008, I finally realized what my role was in the aircraft accident. I was a "path finder." My survival instinct led me to move quickly out of my seat after impact, climb out of a hole in the fuselage onto the left wing of the burning 747, drag the woman on the wing in the blue pantsuit away from the fire and jump off the wing, all in a matter of 40 seconds or so. It was up to other people to follow me out of the aircraft. Four of my fellow passengers made the choice to follow me out of the plane. Almost solely because of their choice or decision, they survived as well. I am so gratified that I was able to help someone while ensuring my own survival. I know that if I had changed seats before we taxied out for takeoff I would not be here. And those other four people would not have survived either. I doubt that I would have survived if I stayed inside the plane to help other people escape the fire. I know of one person who died in that endeavor and have recently read of another one who died in the same valiant effort.

My advice for other people who find themselves in a similar situation is always the same. Get up and get out! Never wait for the fire truck. Never! Don't count on the flight attendants to get you out of the plane. Three of them were sitting right behind me and they did not survive. Follow directions if there are any. You are on your own. Your survival is up to YOU!

One of my co-walking survivors, Enid Tartikoff, told us that she did not want to get out of her seat after the impact. She wanted to wait for the firemen to get into the plane to rescue her. Her husband, Jordan, physically, had to move her hands out of the way, open her seatbelt and pull her out of her seat. Then they jumped out of a hole in the side of the fuselage to the ground.

The smoke from an aircraft fire can be very toxic. Current rules governing the interior fabric in aircraft stipulate that they have to be nontoxic if they catch on fire. Don't count on it. The smoke itself will cause a person to stop breathing if enough smoke is inhaled during a fire inside a plane. Never wait for the fire truck! Get up and get out!

My father told me a story of a co-worker of his who had to make an emergency evacuation out of an airplane. Several months after the accident in Tenerife they were lined up for takeoff in Honolulu when one of the engines began to smoke. There was no fire but the air conditioning system brought the smoke inside the plane. The wife got to an exit door before the flight attendant arrived. Once the door was open and the escape chute deployed, she was the first one out of the plane. Her husband stayed on the plane as he was convinced that there was no fire and relayed that to other passengers. He was among the last passengers off the smoke filled plane.

Most people have goals in life. Some goals are short term and others are long term. Since the accident, I have been giving a piece of advice to everyone I meet and I repeat it here for all to read: If there is something that you would like to do in your lifetime, make an effort to complete that goal or task now, for tomorrow is not promised to anyone.

Most of the passengers on the last flight of Pan Am Clipper Victor were over sixty years of age. I was among the younger group of people on the plane, other than the flight attendants. Several years before the accident, I decided that I wanted to see various places around the world that I had read about or seen on television or in the movies. I chose to live cheaply so I could travel.

I did not want to wait until my later years to travel outside of the United States. In my early twenties I traveled with my parents and siblings to Hawaii and that piqued my interest further in exploring the world. A couple of years after that I went on a cruise through the Caribbean. That created an interest in exploring the civilizations surrounding the Mediterranean Sea. I almost died on that trip but I didn't. I refused to live in fear.

I wanted to see some places in Europe that had caught my attention. In the early eighties I visited West Germany twice as well as England, Holland and France. I have been as far east of the United States as Russia and as far west as China. The farthest south I have travelled is Australia. The northernmost spot I have visited is Norway.

I still get excited when I think of traveling. It's fun to think of a destination, then plan the trip. The trip is usually booked several months in advance so the anticipation builds over several months. Finally, the departure date arrives and off I go! It is so much fun!

↶ Chapter 21 ↷

EPILOGUE

The Canary Islands aircraft accident remains the worst aviation accident in world aviation history. Many writers and video producers have mentioned the accident that occurred on March 27, 1977, and point to it as the prime example of what can go wrong on the ground. As a survivor and one who has documented what happened that day with photographs, I want all aviation professionals to revisit what happened that foggy Sunday afternoon. I want them to recognize the potential for this to happen again and to stop the chain of events that can lead to a collision on the ground like this one. Air traffic controllers can put as many aircraft on a taxiway as they want but there must only be one aircraft on a runway at any given time. I want pilots to be aware of unusual maneuvers or instructions. I also want travelers to keep the pressure on lawmakers and regulators to constantly identify problems in the aviation industry and resolve them.

I believe that the largest audience for my book is comprised of anyone who has been a passenger on a commercial aircraft, like myself. I place a great deal of trust in the mechanics and pilots who maintain and operate aircraft and the controllers who direct them on the ground and in the air. I am confident that the flight attendants can take care of us in an emergency, not just provide us with food and drinks. I feel that these professionals have been trained and certified in their field of expertise and I have full confidence in them. With the technology currently available and the communication training provided, we expect to travel safely to our destination. Aviation has always been an endeavor of innovation and improvement. The new technology that will arrive in the next few years, Automatic Dependent Surveillance Broadcast, will greatly enhance aviation safety, especially on the ground. I look forward to its mandatory operational date of January 1, 2020.

Even before I began to write my story of surviving the Canary Islands aircraft accident, I knew that I wanted to locate and communicate with our co-pilot that day in Tenerife, Pan Am First Officer Bob Bragg. He has become a visible connection to this accident. I had seen his interview in the TV program *Deadliest Crash* and I immediately recognized his voice. In the spring of 2013 I tried again to locate Bob after failing to find him online in several venues. I looked for Pan Am instead and found a website devoted to former Pan Am employees. I typed a message stating who I was and who I was looking for. I wanted to find Bob Bragg and one of the surviving flight attendants, Joan Jackson, who also appeared in Deadliest Crash. I would also like to find the other flight attendant among the group of fourteen walking survivors, Suzanne Donovan.

The next day I got a message from Bob stating, in part, "This is Bob. Call me." With that we made contact and started a conversation. Joan Jackson did not reply, possibly because she may not be involved with the website. Initially, Bob agreed to write something for my book, which then turned into the use of his story. I was quite excited about that prospect. Bob already has written and posted his story on his personal website, http://www.tenerifecrash.com. Bob saw a lot more than I did on that fateful day. After his escape from the burning aircraft by jumping from the flight deck to the ground, he joined all five members of the cockpit crew who walked all the way around the Pan Am 747, looking after survivors and directing emergency response crews to the people who needed them the most. The debris field extended for a long way behind our plane, Bob wrote. Finally, they were taken to Candelario Hospital by a taxicab, as directed by airport authorities.

Eventually, Bob Bragg and I could not come to an agreement over the use of his material in my book. Bob is writing two books in the spring of 2015 and I wish him well in that endeavor. I look forward to reading what he and his wife/editor, Dorothy, have written. I feel confident in writing that both Bob and I agree that this story must be told again, now, to the current generation of aviators. No matter if they work in the cockpit, the cabin, the hangar or in the tower, or are a passenger on a commercial aircraft, we agree that they MUST understand what happened on March 27, 1977 on the island of Tenerife so that this kind of accident never happens again.

I am often asked if I have any contact with any of the other survivors of this accident. As I wrote earlier, I accepted an invitation to meet with fellow survivors Enid Tartikoff and Jim Naik at the American headquarters of the Greek-owned Royal Cruise Lines in San Francisco in late summer of 1977. Enid was a marketing executive and Jim was the chief financial officer of the cruise line at the time. A number of their co-workers joined us for lunch. It was good to see Enid and Jim in a more normal environment. I also met and heard Norm Williams, who was seated directly in front of me in seat 29C on the Clipper Victor. He wrote a book named *Terror at Tenerife* and traveled around the United States giving presentations and selling his book. I attended two of his presentations, first with co-survivors Jim and Elfie Naik and later with a female friend of mine. I have an autographed copy of his book and have found that it is available on Amazon as a used book. It has also been a resource for this book. I tried to find him and was unsuccessful. The publisher of his book does not release any information about any of its authors. I know that Enid passed away in 1994 as I met someone from the local travel industry who attended the service. In the summer of 2014 I spoke on the phone with Jim Naik and his wife, Elfie, who still live in the San Francisco bay area. They remembered me very well and we caught up briefly on our current conditions.

Quite often I happen to meet someone who has a connection to the accident. In the fall of 2014, during my volunteer job as a cashier in the Santa Rosa Sutter Hospice Thrift store, I met a customer who had been a mechanic for Pan Am in San Francisco. Another customer was buying a book about Pan Am's history when the former mechanic approached the counter and happened to see the book. He mentioned that the founder of Pan Am, Juan Tripp, used to walk through the hangar bays often to keep up with what was going on with employees and the aircraft. On another day in the store I was talking with a customer about the accident when a man in line spoke to us. He told us that his roommate in college (University of California at Santa Cruz) was from Santa Cruz de Tenerife, and he said it just like that. I knew immediately that he was familiar with the island. His roommate, who was a young boy in 1977, told him all about the accident. I am sure that it was and still is a big deal there. That conversation was another pleasant surprise for me. I have a desire to return to Tenerife on a book tour. Time will tell if I make it that far.

Also in 2014 while on a trip, I attended an outdoor party. I overheard a conversation in which a man said that he was a pilot. So I walked closer to him and asked him about his flying experience. His first name was also David and he recently retired as a pilot with British Airways, flying the triple seven. I told him that I am a survivor of the Canary Islands accident and he lowered his head and shook it from side to side. Then he looked at me and said that during his last three years with British Airways, he was a CRM Instructor. We both knew what that was about! He was quite amazed to meet someone who was directly involved in that accident and I was interested to meet a teacher of the Crew Resource Management curriculum. As I write, this program was created by National Aeronautics and Space Administration in the United States as a direct result of two U.S. accidents in which jetliners crashed near final approach because no one was monitoring the aircrafts' performance and the Tenerife accident in which the pilot of KLM refused to listen to his first officer and flight engineer. After my return home from that trip I began to wonder if CRM training programs use any photographs from that fateful day on Tenerife and if some of them are mine. I don't mind if they are using some of my stolen property as this will help to train aviators and others so this type of accident never happens again. Once this book is on the market I expect, and hope, to hear from many people who also have a connection to this accident.

Fewer jumbo jets now are in operation around the world. The airlines have switched to large twin aisle passenger planes, either the Airbus 330 or the Boeing

777. Boeing did not receive a single order for its jumbo 747 jet in all of 2014. Airbus has not received any new orders for its A380 jumbo jet either, but they had about 124 on order, in that same time frame. However, in the summer of that year the Airbus A380 made headlines in the United States. Two non-U.S. airlines began operating that aircraft from their homeland to Dallas, Texas (DFW). Emirates Airlines from Dubai and Qantas from Australia began A380 operation to DFW on the same day. This giant double deck aircraft can carry more passengers, about 525 people in a typical three class seating arrangement, and has a longer range, 9756 miles, than its competitor, the 747. I have read that Qantas Airlines made the switch to the A380 because the 747 does not have enough range to get to the U.S. mainland nonstop. Those 747s departing from Sydney have to stop in northern Australia, usually in Cairns (I've been there) to top off their fuel tanks in order to reach Los Angeles or San Francisco. No U.S. flag airline has placed an order for the A380.

My biggest aviation concern is safety on the ground. There has already been an accident in which a taxiing Airbus A380 clipped the tail of a regional jet, spinning the smaller jet 90 degrees in an instant. There were no injuries, thankfully, and minimal damage to both aircraft. However, because the A380 is so big, special care has to be provided by the flight crew and ground traffic controllers to make sure that aircraft separation on the ground is maintained. I am sure that none of us want to see two of these giant aircraft on the same runway at the same time.

In addition, the Airbus A380 generates a tremendous wake vortex when it takes off. This is wind that is generated by the engines, as hot gasses pass out of them and the wings, as air moves over them. Instead of a straight line wind, the wake vortex from a jet aircraft rolls into a tube—like a horizontal column of air. The wake vortex can cause an airborne aircraft to roll to one side or cause loss of control. The wake vortex dissipates when it reaches the ground but can stay airborne for up to three minutes. The aviation industry became more aware of the dangers of the wake vortex and how long it is present after a crash in New York City. On November 12, 2001, an Airbus A300 jetliner took off from JFK and was airborne when it hit the spiraling air vortex from the previous aircraft, a Boeing 747. In trying to regain control of the aircraft the pilot made a hard adjustment in altitude and the vertical stabilizer broke off, sending the plane to the ground in the Bell Harbor, Queens. There were no survivors.

At the current time, no aircraft is allowed to take off for a full five minutes after an A380 has become airborne. During that time, the airport management sends a crew in a truck onto the runway to look for debris that could endanger other departing aircraft. Those crews have found runway lights and other equipment broken off and lying near the runway. That debris can be fatal, as in the crash of an Air France Concorde that burst into flames and crashed just after takeoff on July 25, 2000. A piece from another aircraft punctured a fuel tank, which caused the fire. The wake vortex from an aircraft is proportional to the size of the aircraft. The larger the aircraft, the more intense and longer lasting the wake vortex.

My other goal with this book is to meet and speak with other remaining survivors of the Canary Islands Aircraft accident. I know that immediately after the accident there were 74 initial survivors and I was in a subgroup of 14 walking survivors who were treated and released from Candelario Hospital. By the week after the Sunday, March 27, 1977 accident, the total number of survivors had declined to 66 and it declined further after that. It is widely reported that 62 people survived this accident but I know that by the sixth week after the accident we lost three survivors who had been badly burned. At that point the real number was 58 and it was expected that one more of us would succumb to injuries. As we approach the thirty-eighth anniversary of the accident in 2015, I want to reach out, first to the other survivors who are still with us, then to the relatives of those who lost their lives because of this accident. The reality of this accident is very close to us. I am 67 on this anniversary year and I am very glad to be here. I was 29 at the time of the accident and almost did not get to be 30. But I did and I feel that I have made good use of my time!

Please remember this. If you are on an airplane on the ground and you see smoke in the cabin, whip off that seat belt, get up and MOVE. Don't wait for instructions. Get up and MOVE. Head for the nearest exit, if it is a safe one. Or find a new one like I did. But most of all, NEVER WAIT FOR THE FIRE TRUCK. It may be too late for you. Get up and MOVE.

How could two of the biggest jetliners in the world run into each other on the ground? It seems impossible but it did happen. I want to do what I can to ensure that this type of aircraft accident never happens again. By reading this book you will help me reach this goal. Thank you for your support.

David Alexander

PART TWO

How the world's deadliest plane crash changed your life.

≽ Chapter 22 ≼

CHANGES IN THE AVIATION INDUSTRY

There are two choices that a person can make after going through a near death event such as surviving a plane crash. A person could withdraw and never fly or travel again. Or they can do what I did, face the threatening activity and conquer the fear of flying for pleasure. I chose not to live in fear. I still want to see other places on this planet and the fastest way to get there is by plane.

Commercial aviation is safer today than at any time in the past. The reported odds are that it is more hazardous to drive to or from any airport than it is to fly on any scheduled commercial flight in the United States and in most of Europe.

Jetliner design has been modified to include a thicker floor or deck. The connection between the seats and the floor has been strengthened to prevent the seats from moving in a survivable accident. A prime example of this occurred in my favorite destination country. American Airlines Flight 331 departed Reagan National Airport in Washington D.C. on December 22, 2009, with a scheduled stop in Miami, Florida, then continued to the capitol of Jamaica, Kingston. The flight crew attempted to land in a heavy rainstorm and landed long, meaning the plane landed far down the runway. They "ran out of asphalt", ran off the end of the runway, continued across a road and came to rest on a beach. The fuselage was cracked, the right engine came off and the left main landing gear collapsed. There was no fire. The cabin crew evacuated all of the passengers with NO fatalities. Part of the reason for all persons on board Flight 331 surviving was that everyone stayed in their seat during impact and the seats remained attached to the floor.

The accident in Tenerife caused a major seismic shift in aviation safety. Governments, pilot groups and airlines worked together to develop and implement a new dynamic relationship in cockpit operations. The new operating process is called Crew Resource Management (CRM). At its core is the requirement that one of the two pilots in the cockpit be flying the plane or monitoring the autopilot processes at all times. This has become even more important with the current generation of commercial jetliners because the role of the flight engineer has been automated. The flight engineer's position has been designed out of the airplane and replaced with detailed information about the engine's performance and flight information in a digital format as viewed on a multifunction display mounted in the center of the dashboard, so that both pilots can readily access and view the information.

Failure to follow the procedure has been noted in the news media recently. I am aware of two instances in which neither of the pilots was monitoring the autopilot performance of the plane. The plane flew over the destination airport and kept on going. The air traffic controllers in the tower tried to contact the plane as they were expecting the aircraft to land at their airport. In one case, the aircraft in question was flying from the west coast of the United States to our island state of Hawaii. As the plane flew over the airport without any contact from the flight crew the air traffic controller was able to send a signal to the cockpit that caused a high pitched squeal. The pilots responded to the noise and immediately began to monitor the radio and check their navigation information. They turned off the autopilot system, turned the plane around and with radio contact with the controllers, were given priority in the landing sequence. They still had enough fuel onboard to land safely as the requirement is to have enough fuel to fly for one hour beyond the intended destination. I'm not sure what happened to those specific pilots but you can be sure that, at the minimum, they were ordered to take some retraining in CRM.

The more recent incident concerned a flight that was approaching an airport in northeast United States. As the plane overflew its destination airport, the air traffic controllers in the tower tried to make radio contact with the pilots, but were unsuccessful. Then the airlines management office got involved. One of the staff in that office had the private cell phone number of a flight attendant who was on board. The flight attendant was contacted and told what was happening. That flight attendant pressed a button that is connected to a very loud buzzer in the cockpit. When one of the pilots responded on the phone, they realized their mistake and quickly turned the plane around and landed safely with assistance from the air traffic controllers. An immediate investigation found that the pilots had violated the first basic rule in Cockpit Resource Management. Both pilots were using their laptop computers, reading a long message from the airline's management team, so that neither one of them was flying or monitoring the aircraft. Both pilots were suspended by the airline according to the news stories.

The other very important detail in Cockpit Resource Management is that the non-flying pilot can challenge the flying pilot, or pilot in command, at any time, about any aspect of operating the aircraft. Both pilots are equals in the cockpit even though the pilot in the left seat usually has more seniority in terms of flight hours than the copilot or first officer. That was a key fault in the Canary Islands accident. The first officer and the flight engineer on the accident's KLM 747 were unable to challenge the pilot sufficiently to get him to stop the unauthorized takeoff.

Also, the Federal Aviation Agency (FAA) has recently made changes to the age rule for the pilots. Up until this rule change by the FAA, all commercial pilots were forced to retire at age 60. As the health of the overall population has improved over time, so has the health of commercial pilots. Pilots get an exhaustive health screening every year. The FAA recently announced that commercial pilots will now be allowed to fly until they are age 65. However, as part of that new rule, any pilot who is over age 60 MUST have a co-pilot who is under age 40. That rule is designed to ensure that at least one of the pilots in the cockpit will be able to perform their duties. In several instances the pilot collapsed for some reason or died in his seat. Each time the co-pilot has been able to land the plane without incident.

Having a senior pilot in the cockpit can be very helpful. I recall an incident with a Boeing 747 also flying from the west coast of the U.S. towards Hawaii. One of the engines failed and shut down. Then in quick succession, two more of the four engines developed a problem and shut down as well. The co-pilot read the data that was coming at them at a rapid pace. He thought the second pair of two engines in question was okay but the fourth engine was malfunctioning. He began to shut down the fourth engine. The pilot stepped in and stopped him. In fact, the second pair of engines had a problem and failed to operate properly. The first officer was about to shut down the fourth engine when the senior pilot realized that the fourth engine was the ONLY one still running. He kept that engine running while the co-pilot tried to restart the second pair of engines. That restart was unsuccessful and the plane continued on to Honolulu on that one engine, as they were beyond the point of no return. All jetliners are designed to fly on just one engine. It cannot takeoff on one engine but, once at altitude, it can fly just fine. That incident shows that having an experienced pilot in the cockpit is very desirable.

The other lesson learned from the Tenerife aircraft accident is that terrorists will use existing infrastructure to cause harm to people. At the time of the accident in the spring of 1977 every major airport had storage lockers that were available to travelers. Bus stations had them as well. Some were made of wood and others were metal structures. They usually had three rows of storage spaces from top to bottom and could be configured in a horizontal row as long as the operator wanted. They could be bolted together in any reasonable length. Each locker was large enough to hold a large suitcase. They were coin operated and had a key lock. Each locker had a number on the door with a key in the lock with the same locker number on it. A coin inserted in a slot kept the storage space locked for a certain period of time, usually one hour. The customer turned the key and then removed it to secure the locker.

A terrorist group from northern Spain has been fighting the Spanish government for a long time. The group wants to form a separate country in northeastern

Spain and southwestern France and is known as Euskadi Ta Askatasuna (acronym of ETA). Instead of following a democratic process of qualifying a ballot measure for voters to decide the issue, this group resorted to violence. They decided to target the Canary Islands, a possession of Spain. When the bomb exploded on Sunday March 27, 1977, in a storage locker at the Las Palmas airport, the airport management team decided to close the airport to all incoming flights immediately. All flights were then diverted to the neighboring island of Tenerife. Just before or just after the bomb exploded in the airport terminal, airport authorities received a call claiming responsibility for the bombing on behalf of the separatist group ETA. He indicated that there was another bomb in the terminal. A subsequent search of the airport and its lockers found no other explosive device. After authorities were certain that no other explosive was on site, they reopened the airport to traffic.

The Basque separatist group ETA did not intend to cause the worst aviation accident in world history. However, their action that fateful day led to this accident and the tremendous loss of life to 544 people with injury to the 74 initial survivors. Airport operators and regulators around the world soon recognized the real hazard presented by coin-operated storage lockers. Within months after the accident, storage lockers were permanently removed from almost every airport around the world. The ground transportation industry followed the lead of the airports and removed them from their premises as well.

I remember that there was an explosion in a locker at Gunn High School in Palo Alto around this time. The blast damaged the locker in which the explosive device was housed. No one was injured in the blast but severe repercussions were felt around the country. At the next school board meeting it was decided to remove all lockers from the school grounds. That explosion could be noted as the bomb heard around the world. School boards around the United States followed Gunn High School's action and removed their schools' lockers as well. That's why school children all over the United States, if not the world, have to carry ALL of their books with them all the time. All of those changes in local schools were the indirect result of the bombing in the Las Palmas airport which led to the accident on Tenerife.

I have a great deal of confidence in the success of any flight operating in North America and Europe. Flying on a scheduled carrier has never been safer than it is now. Some other places in the world have a higher risk of flight failure, especially in Africa. Consult with a travel agent if you have questions about the risk of flight operations outside of those two areas.

Another aviation industry change after our accident was the modification of aircraft radios so that when two radios transmit at the same time, they can be heard by other receivers. The Los Rodeos airport tower asked Pan Am to tell the tower when they were clear (of the runway). Pan Am transmitted at the same time which resulted in a squeal in the audio, which rendered the message inaudible.

That phenomenon is called a heterodyne. Because of that particular heterodyne, KLM only heard Pan Am say "we are clear" instead of the full message, "Will report when we are clear." That communication gap failed to inform the KLM cockpit crew that the Pan Am 747 was still on the main runway. That, in turn, led KLM to initiate a takeoff run in spite of not having clearance from the tower.

All aviation process improvements in manufacturing and operations result from mishaps, failures or research. Aviation personnel, with instruction from the governing agency, modify, test and validate processes used to build or operate aircraft.

∾ Chapter 23 ⊰

COULD AN ACCIDENT LIKE TENERIFE HAPPEN AGAIN? YES IT HAS.

The technical term for the accident that occurred in the Canary Islands is runway incursion. An incursion occurs any time two aircraft occupy the same space at the same time. If it occurs in the air it is called a midair collision. If it happens on the ground it is called a runway incursion. Incursions do not have to involve two aircraft. It could and has involved one aircraft that collided with another vehicle, such as a truck, on the ground. Could it happen again? Definitely yes and it has happened again.

I remember going to a meeting at the Ballena Bay Yacht Club in Alameda in early 1991. It was a Friday evening and I had a little time before I left my home in Palo Alto to watch part of the evening news on television. The first item was a report from Las Angeles International Airport (LAX) about a fatal collision on the ground between two passenger airliners. A Boeing 737 was landing when a small propeller driven Fairchild Swearingen Metroliner commuter plane pulled on to the active runway right in front of the 737. The commuter plane was completely crushed when the larger 737 landed in top of it. The 737 lost directional control, careened off the runway and collided with a building. Many people died in the ensuing fire on the 737. The captain was pinned in the cockpit and could not be extracted by firefighters.

When I arrived at the clubhouse I began chatting with my friend, Martha Kidd, who later married Bruce McDivit. Martha was and still is a flight attendant for Delta Airlines. She was based at LAX at the time. I told her about the accident, then we stood in front of the TV, holding hands, watching this story unfold. She tightened her grip as we watched in horror! The commuter plane had been cleared by a ground controller to enter a taxiway which was parallel to the active runway. Instead the commuter plane taxied on to the active runway. Martha realized right away that the accident could have involved a plane on which she was serving.

The subsequent investigation showed that the ground controller did not and could not see the gate where the commuter plane was docked nor could they see the taxiway. The controllers counted on the pilots to tell them where they were. The Federal Aviation Administration subsequently installed a camera system to monitor that blind spot. That accident is another one that has had a lasting impact on me.

Martha currently lives in Savannah, Georgia with her husband Bruce and flies with Delta out of Hartsfield International Airport in Atlanta.

Just months after the Tenerife incursion, I was reminded once again how fragile life can be. On September 25, 1978, a midair collision over San Diego shook me to the core. A Pacific Southwest Airlines (PSA) 727 flying from Los Angeles (LAX), as Flight 182, on a short hop to San Diego, collided midair with a Cessna 172 general aviation aircraft while on final approach to Lindbergh Field in San Diego. I heard about this accident on the evening news that night. Air traffic control was in touch with PSA 182 and told them about the Cessna 172 flying in the same direction at three thousand feet. The captain told ATC that he had the Cessna in visual contact. (The cockpit tapes revealed that neither pilot actually saw the small Cessna.) There was a loud bang and the Boeing 727 rolled slightly to the right in a nose down attitude. The collision occurred at about 2,600 feet and both aircraft crashed to the ground moments later. One hundred and forty-four people lost their life that morning, including Flight 182's seven crew members, 30 additional PSA employees deadheading to PSA's San Diego base, the two Cessna occupants, both of whom had multiple FAA licenses and seven people on the ground. In addition, seven people on the ground were injured. (At the time, this accident was the deadliest aviation accident in the U.S. and remains the worst one in California.)

The accident over San Diego affected me a great deal. I thought about the passengers on board that day. Based upon my experience in Tenerife I felt that the terror that they experienced caused some of them to black out so they felt no pain upon impact. However, the professionals on board did know what was happening and probably died wide awake. One of the pilots said goodbye to his mother. Either way, it was a horrible accident and I still think about it today. My sympathy always goes to the survivors. In this accident, there were none.

Chapter 24

IMPROVEMENTS IN AIRCRAFT INTERIOR SAFETY

ircraft interior safety includes fire safety. The FAA has mandated numerous changes to the types of fabric and fiberglass/plastic materials that are installed inside of today's aircraft. All of these changes are the result of accidents on the ground and one airborne fire incident in particular. Fire on an aircraft that is airborne is a horrendous anomaly that most passengers do not think about. Equipment is in place now to deal with that threat. This was not always the case.

Most regulations regarding safety and operation of commercial aircraft come into force because of an accident or incident on an aircraft. Fire on an aircraft in flight does not happen very often but once it did happen the regulators took action. The regulators were required to develop criteria and tests to prove that the proposed changes they planned would have the intended result.

As a result of a cabin fire in a DC-9 jetliner operated by Air Canada in 1983, regulators in North America and Europe mandated the installation of fire suppression equipment on all aircraft in operation at that time. The regulators also required that all material in a cabin's interior be fire resistant and not give off toxic smoke in case of an onboard fire. These rules were extended to new aircraft in production at that time. I have some experience with fire and toxic smoke inside an aircraft!

The Federal Aviation Administration (FAA) in the United States issued new rules and regulations starting in the mid 1980's that addressed the issue of fire on board commercial aircraft. My editor, Diane Nelson Abel, found a graphic from the FAA that notes a list of fire related safety issues and the required changes to aircraft interiors. I have developed information that supports each of the required changes to aircraft interiors.

The Federal Aviation Administration in the United States was required by

Congress to develop regulations that led to improved fire prevention onboard an aircraft. Industrial chemical companies created and developed materials that suppressed fire inside an aircraft. The FAA developed tests to determine how a material would behave in an aircraft fire. They could not arbitrarily order changes to the interior of commercial aircraft. All proposed changes had to be tested to prove that the material in question does perform as required. I invite the reader to read the details of how this was accomplished.

An airborne fire in 1983 was the catalyst that led to the changes in the interior materials used in commercial aircraft. Over a period of six years the FAA mandated changes that improved crew and passenger safety by reducing the possibility of fire and the resulting smoke on commercial aircraft. Improvements were made in the evacuation alerting system that allowed passengers to find their way to an exit door in the presence of smoke in the cabin. The government and industry learned that if the passengers remained in their seats during a hard landing they had a very good chance of surviving. In 1988 the FAA mandated improved seats that could withstand 16G's of force instead of 9G. Since then, the government and industry have worked together to strengthen the floor in the cabin and the connector between the seats and the floor.

Aviation has always been an industry of trial and error. In modern times the trial takes place inside a laboratory, in a controlled, documented system that measures the results of all tests. The tests are designed in detail and then closely monitored for results.

I was familiar with the inflight fire on a Canadian flag carrier in the 1980's. However, I thought the fire was caused by a passenger who violated the no smoking rule and discarded a cigarette into the trash bin in the lavatory. Research showed that this was not the case. This is what actually happened.

Air Canada Flight 797 was a scheduled trans-border flight that flew on a Dallas/

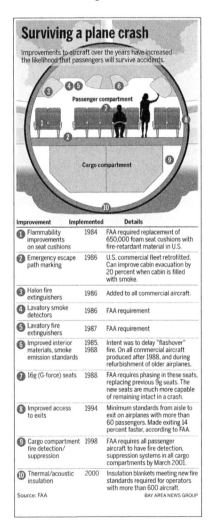

Surviving a plane crash

Improvements to aircraft over the years have increased the likelihood that passengers will survive accidents.

Passenger compartment

Cargo compartment

Improvement	Implemented	Details
1 Flammability improvements on seat cushions	1984	FAA required replacement of 650,000 foam seat cushions with fire-retardant material in U.S.
2 Emergency escape path marking	1986	U.S. commercial fleet retrofitted. Can improve cabin evacuation by 20 percent when cabin is filled with smoke.
3 Halon fire extinguishers	1986	Added to all commercial aircraft.
4 Lavatory smoke detectors	1986	FAA requirement
5 Lavatory fire extinguishers	1987	FAA requirement
6 Improved interior materials, smoke emission standards	1985, 1988	Intent was to delay "flashover" fire. On all commercial aircraft produced after 1988, and during refurbishment of older airplanes.
7 16g (G-force) seats	1988	FAA requires phasing in these seats, replacing previous 9g seats. The new seats are much more capable of remaining intact in a crash.
8 Improved access to exits	1994	Minimum standards from aisle to exit on airplanes with more than 60 passengers. Made exiting 14 percent faster, according to FAA.
9 Cargo compartment fire detection/suppression	1998	FAA requires all passenger aircraft to have fire detection, suppression systems in all cargo compartments by March 2001.
10 Thermal/acoustic insulation	2000	Insulation blankets meeting new fire standards required for operators with more than 600 aircraft.

Source: FAA BAY AREA NEWS GROUP

Fort Worth-Toronto-Montreal route. On 2 June 1983, the aircraft developed an in-flight fire behind the washroom that spread between the outer skin and the inner decor panels, filling the plane with toxic smoke. A passenger reported smoke in a lavatory to a flight attendant. Senior Flight Attendant, Sergio Benetti, 37, used a handheld fire extinguisher to put out a fire in the lavatory trash receptacle, at the request of Flight Attendant Judi Davidson, 33, who was the first crew member to investigate the fire. The cockpit was contacted and the captain, Donald Cameron, 57, sent the first officer, Claude Ouimet, 34, back to investigate. First Officer Ouimet determined that the fire was more than paper burning in the trash receptacle. He returned to the cockpit after three minutes and urged the captain to land immediately.

The fire continued to burn and send smoke into the cabin. Since the plane was not full, flight attendant Laura Kayama moved the passengers forward to empty seats to get them away from the fire. The spreading fire burned through crucial electrical cables that knocked out most of the instrumentation in the cockpit. Captain Cameron made a difficult straight in emergency landing in Cincinnati, Ohio. Ninety seconds after the plane landed and turned off the runway the doors over the wing were opened. The heat of the fire and fresh oxygen from the open exit doors created flashover conditions, and the plane's interior quickly became engulfed in flames, killing 23 of the 41 passengers who had not yet evacuated the aircraft. All of the crew members survived.

The accident investigation found that a water pump, associated with the toilet, overheated, which melted the insulation on the wires of the pump, which, in turn, started a fire in the acoustic thermal insulation that is between the outer fuselage skin and the inner cabin walls. There was no way the cabin crew could have gained access to that fire to put it out.

Because of this accident, aviation regulations around the world were changed to make airplanes safer, with new requirements to install smoke detectors in lavatories and emergency lighting leading to exit doors, plus increased fire fighting training and equipment for crew members. Regulators also mandated that automatic fire suppression equipment be installed on aircraft with the nozzles pointed to potential fire ignition sources.

While doing research on this accident, I learned that the airline, Air Canada, had another DC-9 that had wing damage but was flyable. The airline obtained a ferry permit (no passengers allowed) and flew that aircraft to Cincinnati where airframe and power plant technicians had removed the wings of the fire damaged aircraft. The technicians then replaced the damaged wings on the damaged aircraft with the good wings from the fire damaged aircraft. The rebuilt aircraft then served Air Canada for several years.

1. Flammability improvement on seat cushions. 1984

The Federal Aviation Administration adopted a rule in 1984 that all seat cushions in passenger aircraft had to have a fire retarding covering over the foam cushion. The foam itself is a fire hazard and gives off toxic fume when it burns. However, the FAA found that if the foam pad has a fire blocking material around it, the foam will not burn.

The Federal Aviation Administration conducted tests on fabric and foam at the William J. Hughes Technical Center which is located at the Atlantic City New Jersey International Airport. The Fire Safety Section developed the test methods to prove that the ideas developed by them actually worked and the standards which are used to measure results were valid.

Laboratory fire tests were developed and conducted, then expanded by the Fire Safety Section at the technical center to full scale tests using fuselages of old aircraft. The Air Canada fire was a wake-up call to regulators about the problem with foam in aircraft seats. The mass of foam inside an aircraft was soon realized to be a major factor in a cabin fire. Heat radiation from a fire will pass through the outer fabric layer of the cushion and ignite the foam inside. The burning foam then gives off smoke and toxic fumes and in turn, feeds the fire with more material. The key to stopping this deadly chain of fire was to keep the foam from igniting. Tests completed at the technical center proved that the thin layer of fire blocking material protected the foam padding which prevented fire from spreading through the cabin.

2. Emergency escape path marking. 1986

In 1986 the Federal Aviation Administration issued more aircraft interior fire safety requirements. In an effort to make it possible for passengers to find their way out of a smoke filled cabin that may be on fire the agency added a requirement in 1986. In addition to the illuminated emergency exit signs above exit doors, manufacturers and airlines were required to add an emergency lighting system on the floor which leads to exit doors. The floor proximity lighting system had to be independent of the main lighting system and several other requirements were added including that all lights had to be illuminated during an evacuation.

Several lighting manufacturing companies provided many types of lighting systems for testing by the FAA. All of them met the requirements of the agency so the manufacturers and the airlines were able to choose an approved vendor and install the lighting system.

3. Halon Fire Extinguishers. 1986

Halon fire extinguishers were required in all commercial aircraft beginning in 1986. The FAA and other governments were still responding to the Air Canada airborne fire of 1983. Halon is a liquefied, compressed gas that stops the spread of fire by chemically disrupting combustion. The gas is rated for class "B" fires (flammable liquids) and class "C" fires (electrical) but it is also effective on Class "A" fires (common combustibles). Halon is a "clean agent" that is electrically non-conductive and does not leave a residue upon evaporation.

Halon, however, was found to be an ozone depleting chemical and its production was banned in 1986. The U.S. Environmental Protection Agency has recognized that Halon remains the most effective "clean" extinguishing agent available. There are no U.S. federal or state regulations that prohibit the purchase, sale or use of Halon extinguishers. All Halon available now is recycled so it is an environmentally responsible choice.

Research for an environmentally acceptable replacement for Halon has been ongoing since the late 1990's. In early 2002 two agents passed the Minimum Performance Standards (MPS) and were accepted by the U.S. government. One of these is non-halon lavex—HFC-227ea—and has been installed in all in-production Boeing aircraft starting in 2006. However, this is an incremental replacement because it is classified as a hydroflourocarbon (HFC) which is defined by the Kyoto Protocol as a greenhouse gas and may be subject to future restrictions.

4. Lavatory Smoke Detectors. 1986

The FAA issued rules in 1986 that required smoke detectors on all aircraft that can carry 20 or more passengers. The detectors are connected to a warning system that is monitored at a flight attendant station or the cockpit and provide a light or an audible warning. Each lavatory must have a built-in fire extinguisher that discharges automatically.

It is hard to imagine now that people were allowed to smoke in the airport terminal, at the gate and onboard an aircraft. Finally, public opinion and the U.S. Congress put restrictions in place that completely banned smoking inside a commercial aircraft. Most airports in the United States have smoking rooms in the terminals beyond the security checkpoints. The air conditioning for those rooms is completely separate and independent of the system for the rest of the building. I understand that the filters for those smoking rooms are changed frequently and turn black and yellow because of the tar and nicotine in the tobacco products.

As I wrote earlier about the scene at the gate at Los Angeles International Airport (LAX), on March 26, 1977, Enid Tartikoff, an executive with Royal Cruise Lines, was walking around the gate area with the chef from the ship. She was introducing him to passengers and explaining that he had been in California for a short period of time to learn some of the dishes that Americans like to eat. I am sorry that I do not remember his name but he was smoking most of the time he spent with Enid. Also, the cruise line assigned all of the seats on the plane based on answers to a questionnaire. One of the questions was: do you smoke? All of the smokers were assigned seats in the back of the plane, possibly except for some of the passengers in first class.

How and why was smoking banned on commercial flights in the United States? It wasn't easy but the rule of law changed when enough people spoke up and demanded change. On February 25, 1990, the "no-smoking" sign was permanently lit on U.S. domestic airline flights. Thanks to the hard work of flight attendants and key lawmakers, U.S. airline employees and passengers have been breathing smoke free air since then. Listed below are the dates when smoking was banned on U.S. domestic flights.

1979: Cigars and pipes banned on aircraft
1988: Smoking banned on U.S. Domestic flights under 2 hours
1990: Smoking banned on U.S. Domestic flights under 6 hours
1998: Smoking banned on all U.S. Domestic flights
2000: Federal law introduced banning smoking on all flights by U.S. airlines.

5. Lavatory Fire Extinguishers. 1987

Each lavatory compartment on aircraft is outfitted with a fire extinguisher system that extends into the paper waste compartment. Each extinguisher has two nozzles extending from the bottle into that compartment. The bottle contains pressurized Halon 1301 or an equivalent fire extinguishing agent. When the temperature in the waste compartment reaches approximately 170 degrees F, the solder that seals the nozzles melt and the Halon is discharged.

The disposal receptacles themselves must comply with the requirements of FAR 14 CFR 25.853 (f) which states:

Each receptacle used for the disposal of flammable waste material must be fully enclosed, constructed of at least fire resistance materials, and must contain fires likely to occur in it under normal use. The ability of the receptacle to contain those fires under all probable conditions of wear, misalignment, and ventilation expected in service must be demonstrated by test.

The MPS (Minimum Performance Standard) for lavatory trash receptacles was the first to be completed and published because of the relative simplicity of this application. In late 2000, an FAA/Boeing team conducted tests in accordance with the MPS at the FAA Technical Center in New Jersey. Two environmentally acceptable halon replacement agents, HFC-236fa and HFC-227ea, passed the MPS tests. Boeing has reported that it is currently offering lavatory extinguishers containing these agents to its customers. In addition, Airbus has reported that they selected HFC-236fa, and that lavatory extinguishers charged with HFC-236fa are available for installation on new production aircraft and in-service aircraft as well.

These tests and new standards are the direct result of the Air Canada Flight 797 in-flight fire as noted earlier. The fire extinguisher systems originally designed for lavatory service were extended to the toilet pump assembly area and later to the cargo bay of the aircraft.

6. Improved Interior Materials 1985, Smoke Emission Standards 1986

The Federal Aviation Administration issued new rules in the mid 1980s that were designed to delay the start of a flashover cabin fire like the one that struck Air Canada Flight 797. That plane made a successful emergency landing in Cincinnati, Ohio, with smoke in the cabin. As soon as the cabin doors were opened, however, the air rushing into the cabin created a flashover fire that caused the deaths of 23 people.

The FAA and aircraft manufacturers worked together to develop and test aircraft interiors that met the new requirements. An in-flight cabin fire fortunately was a very infrequent occurrence. However, the absolute terror of that led the regulators to develop systems that almost completely eliminate that possibility.

Two types of fires can affect an airplane and its occupants: in-flight and post-crash. An in-flight fire usually occurs as a result of a system or component failure or maintenance issue. A post-crash fire usually results from ignition of fuel released during a crash landing. Aircraft manufacturers consider both types of fires when designing for airplane cabin fire protection. Fire protection is one of the highest considerations in airplane design, testing, and certification.

In designing an airplane's fire protection features, aircraft manufacturers use a systems-level approach that goes beyond ensuring individual parts meet fire property requirements by looking at the integration of all those parts on the airplane. This approach uses the principles of material selection, separation, isolation, detection, and control. These principles involve separating the three contributory factors to a fire (fuel, ignition source, and oxygen), isolating potential fires from spreading to other parts of the airplane, and controlling a fire should one occur. Manufacturers use both passive systems (such as the use of noncombustible or self-extinguishing materials) and active systems (such as fire extinguishing systems).

Most materials used in the construction of passenger compartment interiors are required by the U.S. Federal Aviation Administration (FAA) to be self-extinguishing (i.e., stop burning after the flame source has been removed) or better. For example, electrical wire and cable insulation must be self-extinguishing after 1985. The interior components of the aircraft were tested to make sure they met the new standards. Components include: Interior ceiling and sidewall panels, cabin partitions, galley surfaces and structure which include exposed surfaces of stowed galley carts and standard galley containers, large cabinets and cabin baggage stowage compartments and passenger seat material. The FAA developed test standards that were used to test the various components of an aircraft's interior.

In 1985, the FAA developed a new test standard for large surface area panels, such as ceilings, walls, overhead bins, and partitions. The standard required that all commercial airplanes produced after August 20, 1988, use panels that exhibit reduced heat and smoke emissions, delaying the onset of a flashover (i.e., the simultaneous or near-simultaneous ignition of all flammable material in an enclosed area). Interiors are updated and refurbished many times during the life of an airplane. This results in interiors that incorporate these enhancements even in older airplanes.

In addition, airplanes manufactured on or after August 20, 1990, must comply with definitive standards of a maximum peak heat release rate of 65 kilowatts per square meter, and specific optical smoke density of 200 (i.e., the OSU 65/65/200 fire safety standard defined by Ohio State University).

Extensive fire protection systems are part of every commercial passenger airplane. These systems include the use of fire-protective materials, smoke detection and fire extinguishing systems, and insulation blankets designed to resist burn-through from a fuel fire next to the bottom half of the fuselage.

Ongoing work with regulators has resulted in interiors that are designed to increase the survivability of accidents that occur during takeoff or landing.The accident fatality rate for jet airplanes has fallen dramatically during the last 50 years. This decrease is due in part to continuing efforts by airplane manufacturers and regulators to use information gained from accidents to develop safer, more survivable airplanes. The following article is used courtesy of the Boeing Corporation:

A HISTORY OF IMPROVING AIRPLANE INTERIORS

Since the first passenger airplane was introduced in the 1930s, airplane manufacturers have worked to make airplanes safer for the passengers and crew who fly in them. For example, Boeing has worked continuously to enhance the safety of its products and to lead the industry to higher levels of safety through global collaboration. By working together, regulators, operators, and manufacturers can maximize safety by sharing knowledge and targeting safety efforts to address areas with the most risk.

Some recent events highlight the safety of today's passenger jet airplane interiors during takeoff and landing accidents.

•   In December 2008, an airplane crashed while taking off, ending up on fire in a 40 foot deep ravine several hundred yards from the runway. There were no fatalities among the 115 passengers and crew, even though the metal fuselage had been breached by fire.

•   In December 2009, an airplane carrying 154 passengers and crew overran the runway during a landing in heavy rain and broke apart. There were no fatalities.

•   In August 2010, an airplane crashed while attempting to land during poor weather, breaking into three pieces on impact. There were 125 survivors among the 127 passengers and crew aboard the flight.

The industry's work on airplane safety and survivability of airplane interiors emphasizes three areas: surviving impact, surviving a fire, and evacuation.

Survivability is greatly influenced by seat design. The greater the ability of airplane seats to remain in place and absorb energy during an impact, the greater the likelihood of passenger survival. In addition, the seat back is designed to protect passengers behind the seat from head injury.

The FAA requires that an airplane can be evacuated of all passengers in 90 seconds. Modern airplane interiors include a number of features to facilitate this process. These features include floor proximity lighting and escape slides. The following graphic illustrates the improvements to aircraft interiors which were mandated by the FAA in the 1980's.

7. 16G (G-force) seats. 1988

The United States Federal Aviation Administration issued rules in 1988 which required newly developed passenger aircraft to have stronger seats installed. Up until that time the seats were required to pass a 9G requirement, which meant that the seat had to hold a passenger in the seat, and the seat remain in place, even if the weight of the passenger increased to 9 times the original weight due to the force of a sudden stop. After October of 2009 the 9G requirement was changed to require a 16G seat meaning the seat had to withstand 16 times the force of gravity. This rule applied to all Part 121 operators, per amendment 121-315, and to all new aircraft manufactured after October 27, 2009. Floors and the tracks on which the seats are connected must also be able to withstand that force. The 9G standard had been in effect since 1952.

The new 16G seats were subjected to a battery of tests to determine their strength, similar to the crash tests that automakers must comply with to meet federal safety standards.

When the FAA proposed the stronger-seat rule in 2002, it envisioned requiring airlines to retrofit existing fleets with the stronger seats. The final rule did not include planes now in service, many of which already have upgraded seats that equal or approximate features of the new, 16G seats.

That change pleased the aviation industry, which argued that retrofitting seats on a regulatory timetable would be too costly. The FAA agreed and concluded that many of the planes with older, weaker 9G seats were retired after the business downturn that followed the Sept. 11, 2001, terrorist attacks. And new aircraft introduced in the 1990s had versions of the updated seats anyway—so-called 16G-compatible seats or neo-16G seats.

Not requiring faster retirement of older seats substantially reduced the cost of the rule. The retrofit would have cost $519 million. The final version of the rule will cost $34.7 million from 2009 through 2034. The FAA estimates that the airlines will take delivery of 1,752 new planes with a total of 225,274 seats during the period—all of which would have to comply with the rule.

The benefits of installing fully compliant seats, calculated on lives saved and injuries averted, total $78.9 million over the same 25-year period. Research done for the FAA showed that 45 fatalities and 40 injuries might have been averted in accidents between 1984 and 1998 if the seats were those called for in the rule.

Aircraft seats are an important part of the equation in making accidents as survivable as possible. Generally the emphasis has been on better protecting the people in an aircraft and getting them out faster. There is no way for a passenger to know what vintage the seat is beneath him.

A 2003 report by the General Accounting Office (now the Government Accountability Office) estimated that at the time, 44 percent of commercial aircraft had full 16G seats, 55 percent were 16G compatible, and 1 percent had 9G seats. Some of the "compatible" seats may offer only minor improvements over the lowest-rated seat, the report said.

"Seat strength is an essential part of crashworthiness," said Nora Marshall, chief of the NTSB's Survival Factors Division in the Office of Aviation Safety. "When a crash begins, there is a lot of energy, and it goes to the ground, fuselage, floor and seats. If the seat breaks loose, you are adding energy."

Marshall said the NTSB has documented crashes in which the seats broke loose and piled up at the front of the plane—even though the type of accident that occurred should have made it a survivable crash.

Thank you to Boeing.

The August 2, 2005, crash landing of an Air France plane in Toronto, Canada, which destroyed an Airbus A-340-300 when it ran off the runway, seems to be an example of the survivability of an airline accident: 12 crewmembers and 297 passengers successfully walked away from the wreck.

A much worse accident than this one happened four years later in Jamaica that made the 16G seats very relevant when a Boeing 737 crash landed in Kingston. On December 22, 2009, the aircraft landed long, ran out of runway, crossed a road, hit an embankment and stopped just short of the Caribbean Ocean. The right engine came off the plane and the landing gear collapsed. Though the fuselage was cracked open in two places, no one died. Why was that? Even though the aircraft was built in 2001, the operator, American Airlines, had installed new 16G seats to improve passenger safety in a hard landing. It was no accident that everyone survived. 16G seats, a stronger floor (deck) and a heavier connector between the seats and the floor ensured that the seats remained in place during this hard impact. With their seatbelts securely fastened the passengers stayed in their seats and suffered no serious injuries.

From the *Observer* newspaper: "Lieutenant Colonel Oscar Derby, director general of the Jamaica Civil Aviation Authority, told the *Observer* newspaper that the "new generation set of passenger seats" carried by the aircraft were constructed to withstand a force, on impact, of 16 times the weight of the passengers seated in them before dislodging.

"While observing the removal of sections of the plane, Derby said that an important part of the investigation would be an assessment of the survivability of the 16G seats. 'There is a very interesting thing about this accident. Those seats you are looking at which are very much intact, are a new generation set of passenger seats which are constructed to withstand 16G-forces—that is an impact which causes the passengers weight to increase by 16 times the normal weight,' he said. 'So a passenger of 200 pounds, on impact, would have to be subjected to a force of 16 times his or her own body weight, or 3200 pounds, before the seat would dislodge.' Director General Derby said the 16G seats replaced 9G seats which were known to detach invariably in an accident and crumple towards the impact end of the accident. That was responsible for a lot of the casualties in air accidents. 'I daresay one could perhaps surmise at this point that the survivability rate [of the 16G seats] is good because all the passengers survived,' he said."

The seats are also said to protect the occupant from debilitating leg and spine injuries; protect crew members from serious chest injury when upper torso restraints are used and ensures that occupants do not become trapped in their seats due to excessive seat deformation.

The aircraft sustained substantial damage during the accident, with the fuselage fracturing forward and aft of the wing, one wing losing an engine and the other its winglet tip, and the nose section being crushed. The landing gear failed, as designed, which put the aircraft on its belly. Its momentum carried it through the perimeter fence at freeway speeds, and across Norman Manley Highway before finally coming to rest, upright, within meters of Kingston's outer harbor and the open Caribbean Sea. The 737 was damaged beyond economic repair.

The accident in Kingston, Jamaica, validates the decision by the FAA to issue

Aerial photo of the runway structure at the Norman Manley International Airport in Kingston, Jamaica. Note that there is water on both ends of the runway. Photo courtesy of Phil Derner Jr., President and Founder, NYC Aviation LLC.

a requirement to install 16G seats in all commercial aircraft. This accident and the Asiana Airlines 777 hard landing in San Francisco on July 6, 2013, clearly shows that the new seats will stay in place during a hard landing, which prevents injuries and save lives.

8. Improved access to exits. 1994

In 1994, the FAA mandated improved the access to Type III exits, by specifying minimum standards for the passageway from the aisle to the exit for airplanes with 60 or more passengers. Type III exits are the non-floor level exit typically located over the wing in thousands of aircraft in air carrier service. Egress rates through the exits were found to be approximately 14% faster than through the earlier allowed narrower passageways. The current size standard for these exits are a rectangular opening of not less than 20 inches wide by 36 inches high with a corner radii of not less than 7 inches, with a step up inside the airplane of not more than 20 inches. If the exit is located over the wing the step-down outside the plane cannot exceed 27 inches.

The emergency escape lighting on the floor of aircraft also direct passengers to the exit doors over the wing. Those doors open inward and are not on a hinge. They come completely out of the fuselage and are placed inside the aircraft in such a way that the door does not block access to the emergency exit. Boeing worked hard to develop a redesigned over-wing exit door for the upgraded 737 NG. The over-wing exit door is attached to the fuselage and rises upward, out of the way when the handle on the door is rotated.

Also, I want to note that no exit door on any aircraft can be opened during flight. The doors automatically lock after takeoff by use of a speed sensitive lock. The locks set automatically when the aircraft reaches a speed that is required for takeoff. The interior air pressure pressing against the door ensures that no person can possibly open a door while the plane is in flight. The math is, with a door of 6 square feet and air pressure inside the aircraft of 2.0 PSI, the force necessary to open an exit door is 1728 pounds. No human can do that even if the door was unlocked. That is why it is impossible to accidently open an exit door while the aircraft is in flight.

9. Cargo compartment fire detection/suppression. 1998

Fire protection is given one of the highest considerations at every aircraft manufacturing company in airplane design, testing, and certification. In designing an airplane's fire protection features, each manufacturer uses the principles of prevention, separation, isolation, and control.

Prevention is the first order of the day, as it is better to prevent a fire than to have to contend with one in flight. The principles involve separating the three essentials for creating a fire: fuel, ignition source, and oxygen, then isolating potential fires from spreading to other parts of the airplane, and controlling a fire should one occur.

To effect this prevention, separation, isolation, and control, the aircraft manufacturers use both passive and active features. Passive features include the use of noncombustible or self-extinguishing materials; separation by routing, compartmentalization, isolation, ventilation, and drainage; and bonding and grounding. Active features include fire and overheat detection systems, fire-suppression systems, temperature sensing, air shut-off means, and automatic shutdown of non-flight critical systems.

The Federal Aviation Administration (FAA) in the United States has identified and classified cargo compartments into three categories.

Class A. The presence of a fire would be easily discovered by a crew member while at his or her station and each part of the compartment is easily accessible in flight.

Class B. There is a separate approved smoke detector or fire detector system to give warning at the pilot or flight engineer station. There is sufficient access in flight to enable a crew member to effectively reach any part of the compartment with the contents of a hand held fire extinguisher. When access provisions are being used, no hazardous quantity of smoke, flames or suppression agent can enter any compartment occupied by the crew or passengers. There are means to control ventilation and drafts within the compartment.

Class C. There is a separate approved smoke detector or fire detector system to give warning at the pilot or flight engineer station. There is an approved built-in fire extinguishing or suppression system controllable from the flight deck. There are means to exclude hazardous quantities of smoke, flames or suppression agent from any compartment occupied by the crew or passengers. There are means to control ventilation and drafts within the compartment so that the suppression agent used can control any fire that may start within the compartment.

In the fall of 2008 the FAA issued an advisory circular that describes an acceptable means to show compliance with the requirements of Title 14, Code of Federal Regulations (14 CFR), part 25, section 25.795(b) "Cargo Compartment Fire Suppression". This section requires that the fire suppression system for the cargo compartment be designed to withstand a sudden and extensive explosion and fire, such as could be caused by an explosive or incendiary device. The means of compliance described in this document provides guidance to supplement the engineering and operational judgment that must form the basis of any compliance findings relative to the design of fire suppression systems for the cargo compartment.

For more details about this fire suppression requirement the reader can easily find the document online.

The National Transportation Safety Board announced recommendations to reduce the harm from fires aboard cargo planes, a move that has been endorsed by a pilots' union. The NTSB can recommend changes to the rules but the FAA is the government agency that controls the rules that all aviation entities must follow. The board urged the Federal Aviation Administration to require fire-suppression systems in all cargo compartments of planes and to improve fire detection within cargo containers and pallets.

"These fires quickly grew out of control, leaving the crew with little time to get the aircraft on the ground," NTSB Chairman Deborah Hersman says. "The current approach is not safe enough."

The recommendations followed three fire-related accidents worldwide. One fire involved a UPS DC-8 which was on the ground in Philadelphia in 2006. Both pilots survived. The second one involved a UPS airborne fire crash in United Arab Emirates in 2010. And a third one involved an Asiana Cargo Jet that crashed into the ocean off South Korea in 2011. The second two fires were fatal accidents.

Safety investigators found that the early stages of a fire burning inside a cargo container often are concealed. Then when a fire grows, it rapidly burns through the container to threaten the plane and crew.

The UPS crash in Dubai killed two crew members aboard a 747-400, whose equipment failed two and a half minutes after the fire was detected. The Asiana fire aboard a 747-400 also killed two crew members. But the two UPS crew members in the Philadelphia fire survived because they were on the ground and exited through the cockpit windows. The DC-8 was destroyed by the fire.

The UPS crash in Dubai was found by that country's Civil Aviation Authority to have been caused by the ignition of lithium-ion batteries, which were carried as cargo. The report in July of 2013 traced the ignition of the onboard fire to a container of those batteries. They have been embraced by consumers because they recharge faster and are smaller than other batteries. But they also tend to overheat and burst into flame. The same type of battery, but of a different size, was found to have been the cause of two fires on board Boeing's new 787 Dreamliner.

Captain Robert Travis, president of the Independent Pilots Association, which represents UPS pilots, thanked the NTSB for its recommendations, by stating "No pilot group is more aware of the tragedy that can result from in-flight smoke and fire than the IPA."

FedEx is installing a fire-suppression system on its long-haul fleet and NTSB Chairman Debora Hersman says UPS briefed her on its efforts.

A UPS spokesman says the company worked with NTSB, FAA and the union to pioneer and test new fire-resistant package containers and covers for cargo on pallets. Experimental suppression equipment sprays a potassium aerosol powder to put out a fire, in an effort to save other packages in the shipment.

In the cockpit, UPS is installing oxygen masks that can be put on quickly, including for the jump seats in 747-400s. On international flights, the company will install inflatable bubbles to ensure pilots can see through smoke to see instruments and out windows. The company is also educating shippers about the safe handling of dangerous products, such as lithium batteries.

In these three cargo aircraft cases, the fires started within the cargo containers aboard the planes, but by the time the plane's fire warning system alerted pilots to the dangers, there was little time for them to react.

Federal regulations require cargo airline fire detection systems to alert pilots within one minute of a fire starting, but the NTSB's investigation found current systems detected fire and smoke anywhere from two and half minutes to more than 18 minutes after the fire started.

The NTSB concluded cargo containers made of flammable materials significantly increase the intensity of the on-board fires because there's been little focus by manufacturers or regulators to develop fire-resistant cargo containers.

Additionally, the NTSB's report recommended improving the fire suppression systems on cargo planes, a recommendation it originally made to the FAA in 2007. After the 2007 recommendation, the FAA did a cost-benefit analysis of upgrading fire suppression systems and found it to be too expensive, a fact the NTSB highlighted in its report.

"The two catastrophic cargo airplane fires that occurred in less than a year occurred after the FAA's cost-benefit analysis concluded that the installation of fire suppression systems was not cost-effective," the board said.

In hindsight, the FAA cost-benefit analysis just looked at the physical attributes of installing a fire suppression system in a cargo aircraft. Therefore, most cargo carriers decided not to install such a system in their aircraft. Since then, at least four crew members on cargo aircraft have lost their lives because they did not have adequate warning that a fire was starting in the cargo bay of their aircraft. What is the cost-benefit ratio now?

10. Thermal/acoustic insulation. 2000

Thermal acoustic insulation blankets are similar in concept to the thermal insulation that is installed in the walls of houses and buildings. However, in addition to keeping cold air out of the structure and warm air inside, the blankets installed in the outer shell of an aircraft also decrease sound from the aircraft exterior and provide a barrier to fire. Aircraft thermal acoustic insulation blankets are sealed on both sides of the blanket. That ensures the integrity of the blanket.

Functions

Both thermal and acoustical insulation are required on passenger aircraft. Historically, both functions have been provided by the same material system, which has mostly been fiberglass batting encapsulated in a plastic pillowcase covering. Covering plastics have been predominantly PET (polyethylene terephthalate) and a lesser quantity of polyvinyl fluoride (PVF). Several companies in the United States manufacture thermal/acoustic insulation for aircraft.

Thermal

The thermal environment outside an airplane produces fuselage skin temperatures from about –60F when in-flight at altitude to about +160F when parked in direct sunlight in the desert. The amount of insulation needed for the air conditioning/heating system to economically produce comfortable cabin temperatures varies with airplane type and location. However, except for a few places such as the crown area over the aft passenger cabin and the lower fuselage area below the passenger floor, acoustic requirements predominate. Therefore, except for those places, the amount of insulation present exceeds that needed for thermal requirements.

Acoustic

Outside aircraft noise is generated by aerodynamics and engines. Insulation is used to attenuate outside noise to allow reasonable levels of comfort and verbal communication inside the passenger cabin and flight deck. The acoustic attenuation needed varies from airplane to airplane, but is generally substantial and insulating material of very high acoustic efficiency is used to minimize the amount (weight, volume) required. Fiberglass batting, using a very small fiber diameter, is a highly efficient acoustic attenuator.

Fire Barrier

Currently, insulation using fiberglass batting will resist fire penetration in lower-intensity thermal environments. Cargo compartments are required to have liners that are fire barriers. In some compartments, the thermal insulation lining the fuselage provides the fire barrier. For these areas, the FAA qualification requirement involves a Bunsen burner test that fiberglass batting easily passes.

The FAA has released information in press reports that it planned to propose a requirement that insulation be resistant to burn through in an intense thermal environment like that of a fuel-fed fire. All insulation material systems would have to be redesigned to meet this requirement.

In 2000 the FAA conducted large number of small-, intermediate-, and full-scale flame propagation tests representative of an in-flight fire. These tests were conducted at the Federal Aviation Administrations' laboratory in the William J. Hughes Technical Center in Atlantic City, New Jersey. The team tested various thermal acoustic insulation blanket materials. Results indicated that the current FAA vertical Bunsen burner test requirement could not adequately discriminate between poorly performing materials and materials that performed well under realistic fire scenarios. A rad radiant panel laboratory test was shown to be an effective method for evaluating the in-flight fire resistance qualities of thermal acoustic insulation.

In addition, a new laboratory test was developed for evaluating the post-crash fire burn through resistance of thermal acoustic insulation. The test method was based on full-scale tests in which a fuselage structure was subjected to jet fuel fires.

Approximately 60 burn-through tests were conducted on a variety of insulation materials. Those insulation materials compliant with the new burn through test method will provide a minimum of four minutes of protection against a post-crash fuel fire, which is the latest FAA requirement.

The Federal Aviation Administration (FAA) has developed new flammability test requirements for aircraft insulation that will result in increased fire safety on aircraft. Special attention is paid to the prevention of onboard fire propagation and fuselage burn-through protection in the event of a post-crash fuel fire. Those new requirements were posted by the FAA on July 31, 2003 and became effective in September of 2003. This rule applied to all new aircraft produced after September 2, 2005.

The change enacted in 2005 calls for the enhancement of the fire-protective features of insulation blankets in the event of an in-flight or post-crash fire. The latest standard increases protection by minimizing the contribution of the insulation blankets to the propagation of a fire. Thermal/acoustic insulation blankets installed behind cabin interior panels with the appropriate fire-resistant properties must delay the onset of fire into the cabin in the event of a crash. The insulation blankets, along with the airplane skin, must be capable of resisting burn-through from a fuel-fed post-crash fire next to the bottom half of the fuselage for a minimum of four minutes to allow passengers to evacuate the airplane before burn-through can occur.

Manufacturing companies involved in the production of thermal/acoustic insulation blankets were made aware of the proposed change in thermal protection and began research and development of an improved blanket. DuPont and Orcon are two American companies that worked on this project to meet new FAA requirements.

In 2002 the DuPont Company developed a polymide film for use in aircraft as a fire protection product. A polymide film is a synthetic polymeric resin of a class resistant to high temperatures, wear and corrosion. Released under the trade name Kapton, the high temperature resistant material does not propagate flame and is not a fire fuel. It will not ignite at extreme high temperatures. The FAA issued an opinion which stated the film can provide a substantial increase in fire resistance over some other insulation covering materials used by the aviation industry.

Other companies have similar products on the market that produce similar results. Orcon Corporation, a leading supplier of aviation insulation, also manufactures a reinforced polyimide covering film, which is the material of choice for improving fire resistance of aircraft insulation. To provide fuselage burn-through protection, a combination of reinforced Kapton® polyimide covering film and new fire-blocking materials can be used. This combination provides burn-through protection for as long as 10 minutes—well over the four minute requirement required by the FAA.

American chemical producer BASF is another company in the forefront of the mission to enhance the fire safety of commercial aircraft. American aircraft manufacturer Boeing is insulating its new airplane series, the Dreamliner 787, with Basotect®, BASF's sound-absorbing and heat-insulating melamine resin foam. This is the first time that a BASF foam is used in the mass production of acoustic thermal insulation for airplane cabin walls and environmental ducting. The outcome of the close cooperation between the two companies is the development of Basotect UL (ultra light), which, at six grams per liter is 30 percent lighter than the conventional Basotect. The companies also developed new test methods for the use of this specialty foam in aviation. Those tests meet FAA standards.

According to Boeing, the lightweight BASF foam supports the company's fuel efficiency targets and, thanks to its high sound-absorbing capacity and its good thermal-insulation properties, Basotect is also instrumental in Boeing's concept for the layout of the Dreamliner 787 series. The new aircraft is quieter than aircraft of a comparable size.

Pieces cut of the elastic melamine resin foam can be installed in the cabin walls easily and quickly. The foam retains its flexibility even at extremely high temperatures as well as at very low temperatures without becoming brittle. In addition, the material is highly flame-retardant, so that Basotect complies with the strict fire-protection standards stipulated by the aviation regulators.

I contacted my friend Mike Smalley, an airframe/power plant technician with Alaska Airlines in Seattle, and asked him about the insulation blankets. My question was "Are the thermal acoustic insulation blankets replaced during the D check inspection process?" The D check is when the entire interior of the aircraft is removed, down to the bare interior bulkhead walls. Mike answered that it is up to the airline, the technician and the inspector as to whether or not the blanket is replaced. The blanket is inspected, then rolled up in place. If no damage is found on the blanket or on the bulkhead, the blanket is then reinstalled. Among the items that the technicians look for are black marks on the insulation blanket. That mark could indicate a burn mark from a wire that is arcing, for instance. The mark can also come from rivets that are loose, overheat then turn black. Repairs to the bulkhead walls are made before the blankets are reinstalled or replaced. The blankets would also be replaced if they were found to have any rips or tears in its outer layer, as that condition would decrease the effectiveness of the blanket.

It would certainly be cost effective for the airlines to reuse the blankets, in my opinion. I feel that this flexibility of the protocol gives the passengers and crew the safety they need and expect.

Aviation is an industry that is constantly changing with new rules and requirements to enhance safety on the ground and in the air. The previous 10 changes, which were mandated by the U.S. Federal Aviation Administration, have greatly improved safety for passengers and crew inside an aircraft. Flying aboard a scheduled commercial aircraft has never been safer than it is right now in 2015. The regulators' current focus is on runway safety to prevent runway incursions like the Tenerife accident. I hope that an accident like that one never happens again.

INTERIOR SAFETY BIBLIOGRAPHY

http://www.plasticsportal.net/wa/plasticsEU~en_GB/portal/show/common/plasticsportal_news/2007/07_429

http://www2.dupont.com/Kapton/en_US/assets/downloads/pdf/aerospace-H-78318.pdf

February 2010
DOT/FAA/AR-TN09/43

http://magazine.sfpe.org/content/research-derived-aircraft-fire-safety-improvements- 2000-2010

FEDERAL AVIATION REGULATIONS
Home > Aviation Regulations > Parts Index > Part 121 > Sec. 121.308 - Lavatory fire protection.

DOT/FAA/AR-00/12
By Arthur L. Tutson, Boeing Organization Designation Authorization, Authorized Representative, Fire Protection;
Douglas E. Ferguson, Technical Safety Chief, Fire Protection, Technical Services and Modifications; and Mike Madden, Deputy Pressurized Compartment Fire Marshal, Payloads Design
By Alan J. Anderson, Payloads Engineering Chief Engineer (Retired), Interiors-Payloads System Engineering
By Robin Bennett, Hazardous Materials Leader, Product Development, Environmental Performance Strategy/Boeing Commercial Airplanes

Cindy Skrzycki *The Washington Post*

Alicia Dunkley *Observer* staff reporter, Jamaica

Carol Hipsher, Senior Manager, Flight Safety and Design Office, Technical Customer Support, and Douglas E. Ferguson, Technical Safety Chief, Fire Protection, Technical Services and Modifications/ Boeing Commercial Airplanes

Richard J. Mazzone, Associate Technical Fellow, Payloads Systems/Boeing Commercial Airplanes

DOT/FAA/AR-99/44

2. Government Accession No. 3. Recipient's Catalog No.

4. Title and Subtitle
DEVELOPMENT OF IMPROVED FLAMMABILITY CRITERIA FOR AIRCRAFT THERMAL ACOUSTIC INSULATION

5. Report Date September 2000

6. Performing Organization Code AAR-422

7. Author(s) :Timothy Marker

AC 25.795-5 – Cargo Compartment Fire Suppression

The Federal Aviation Administration
William J. Hughes Technical Center
Atlantic City New Jersey International Airport

Wiki Answers – Smoking on planes

CNN – Todd Sperry Nov. 29, 2012

Wikipedia – ETOPS

Wikipedia – American Airlines Flight 331

☙ Chapter 25 ❧

IMPROVEMENTS IN RUNWAY SAFETY

A lot has been written about runway safety since the Canary Islands air-craft accident but very little has changed until recently. In 2000, the Federal Aviation Agency (FAA) in the United States created a Runway Safety Council. The new council focused on three types of runway accidents: operational errors by controllers, pilot deviations and vehicle or pedestrian deviations. I want to point out several types of runway incursions and what governments, the regulatory agencies and the aviation industry are doing now to sharply reduce and eliminate this deadly threat. I will write about safety issues on the ground as well as in the air. New technologies are already in use and others in development that will further improve aviation safety.

Research shows that 63% of all aircraft accidents occur at an airport. Most of those accidents occur during the takeoff or landing phase of flight. However, the highest incidents of death on the ground are the result of a runway incursion. A runway incursion is defined as an instance when an aircraft on the ground strikes or collides with an object on the ground. That object could be an aircraft, a ground vehicle or a stationary object like a light pole or a building. The worst type of runway incursion is when an aircraft collides with another aircraft on the ground. In all of the data one can read about this topic, they all state that the worst runway incursion accident in aviation history occurred on March 27, 1977, on the island of Tenerife in the Canary Islands. As you probably have read by now I know a lot about that accident! The drive to improve runway safety has been in place for a long time. Finally, technology has advanced far enough to make this drive a reality. I want to write about what advances are under way now (in 2015) that will greatly improve runway safety and sharply reduce the possibility of an accident like Tenerife from happening again.

What is a Runway Incursion?

The Federal Aviation Administration defines a runway incursion as "any occurrence in the airport runway environment involving an aircraft, vehicle, person or object on the ground that creates a collision hazard or results in a loss of required separation with an aircraft taking off, intending to takeoff, landing or intending to land."

There are four categories of runway incursions:

Category A is a serious incident in which a collision was narrowly avoided.

Category B is an incident in which separation decreases and there is a significant potential for collision, which may result in time critical corrective/evasive response to avoid a collision.

Category C is an incident characterized by ample time and/or distance to avoid a collision.

Category D is an incident that meets the definition of runway incursion such as incorrect presence of a single vehicle/person/aircraft on the protected area of a surface designated for the landing and take-off of aircraft but with no immediate safety consequences.

Different sets of data vary and the language was changed recently to match that of the International Civil Aviation Organization, but somewhere between one and two runway incursions occur every day in the United States, and the potential for a catastrophic accident is "unacceptable," according to the Federal Aviation Administration's risk/severity matrix. The likelihood for runway incursions grows exponentially as a function of air traffic growth. The data collected before and after 9/11 clearly shows this relationship.

In March 1977, in what remains the world's deadliest aviation accident, two passenger jumbo jets collided on a runway at Tenerife, Canary Islands, causing the deaths of 583 passengers and crew. While CRM (Crew Resource Management) and some other actions were born out of that disaster, realization of the runway incursion aspect was not so directly grasped.

The deadliest U.S. runway incursion accident was a collision between a U.S. Air 737 and a Skywest Metroliner commuter airplane at Los Angeles International Airport (LAX) in February 1991, which killed 34 people.

More recently, in July 2006, at O'Hare International Airport in Chicago, a United 737 passenger jet and an Atlas Air 747 cargo airplane nearly collided. The 747 had been cleared to land on 14L and was taxiing on the runway towards the cargo area when the 737 was cleared to take off on the intersecting runway (now called runway 28), over the 747. The pilot of the United 737 passenger jet took off early to avoid a collision with the 747. This collision was avoided by about 35 feet.

The runway incursion issue has been on the National Transportation Safety Board's "Most Wanted" list since that list's inception in 1990, and is one of only two issues that still remains on that original list. The Airline Pilots Association (ALPA) has been pursuing the issue in several venues since before the list began.

Overall, the runway incursion issue is one of the best studied, quantified and documented, and the industry readily knows what needs to be done. The Airline Pilots Association's March 2007 White Paper, entitled "Runways Incursions—A Call for Action" served to catalyze the action currently being undertaken. The association has played an active role for a long time, and is continuing to push the issue forward, for the membership and the travelling public.

The International Civil Aviation Organization (ICAO) on April 27, 2006, defined a runway incursion as:

"Any occurrence at an aerodrome involving the incorrect presence of an aircraft, vehicle or person on the protected area of a surface designated for the landing and take-off of aircraft."

In October 2007, the Federal Aviation Administration dropped its own definition of "runway incursion" and adopted the above. The difference between the two was "that ICAO defines a runway incursion as any unauthorized intrusion onto a runway, regardless of whether or not an aircraft presents a potential conflict—such as an unauthorized aircraft crossing an empty runway—and was defined as a 'surface incident' and not a runway incursion."

The Airport Surface Detection Equipment, Model X (ASDE–X) and the Airport Movement Area Safety System (AMASS) are computerized systems that are intended to alert air traffic controllers to the potential for a runway incursion.

Notable Examples of Runway Incursion

- In the Chicago-O'Hare runway collision, North Central Airlines Flight 575 (a McDonnell-Douglass DC-9) collided during takeoff with Delta Airlines Flight 954 (a Convair CV-880) while the CV-880 was taxiing across a fog-shrouded runway at O'Hare International Airport in Chicago, Illinois, killing 10 people and injuring 17.
- The Tenerife airport disaster in 1977 happened when a plane took off before it was supposed to and collided with another plane.
- On February 1, 1991, U.S. Air Flight 1493 collided with the waiting SkyWest Airlines Flight 5569 on the runway killing 34 people. An air traffic controller mistakenly assigned the inbound flight to a runway where Flight 5569 was waiting to take off.
- 1984 Aeroflot Flight 3352, October 11, 1984: airport maintenance vehicles on the runway while a Tupelov Tu-154B-1 was attempting to land in Omsk, Russia. 174 passengers and 4 people on the ground were killed.
- 1994 TWA Flight 427/Superior Aviation Cessna 441, November 22, 1994: Cessna pilot error at Lambert-St. Louis International Airport. Pilot taxied to the incorrect runway and was struck by the departing TWA MD-80. Two fatalities on

the Cessna.

• On November 16, 1996, United Express Flight 5925 was landing at Quincy Regional Airport when the pilot of a Beech King Air started to take off on an intersecting runway. As the field was uncontrolled, the United Express pilots inquired whether the King Air was clear of the runways. They received no response except for a call from a Piper Cherokee saying they were holding short. The King Air and the United Express collided at the intersection of the two runways killing all twelve on Flight 5925 and the pilot and passenger on the Beechcraft King Air.

• On April 1, 1999, an Air China Boeing 747, Flight 9018, taxied onto an active runway at Chicago's O'Hare International Airport during the takeoff of Korean Air Flight 36, another 747. Flight 36 averts a collision by taking off early, missing the Air China aircraft by 75 feet. There were 8 people on the Air China jet and 379 on the Korean flight.

• T.F. Green Airport runway incursion, December 6, 1999. In low visibility at night, the plane went down the wrong taxiway and ended on the runway just as another plane took off. No collision.

• Linate Airport disaster, October 8, 2001: Milan, Italy. Commercial airliner collided on takeoff with a taxiing Cessna Citation. An MD-87 speeding down Runway 36R for takeoff struck a Cessna Citation Jet, which had entered the runway without clearance at Taxiway R6. There were 114 fatalities.

• Indian Ocean aftermath: Banda Aceh January 4, 2005: water buffalo on runway caused ground collision which seriously delayed relief flights.

Preventing Runway Incursions

Taxi clearances at some large airports are quite complex and subject to misunderstandings.

The objective of Flight Operations Briefing Notes is to provide awareness of a runway incursion, the associated contributing factors and related prevention strategies, especially in terms of best practices for flight crew to avoid runway incursions.

Some of the other definitions of runway incursion are:

1. Inadvertent crossing of a hold-line and/or entry on to an active runway (with or without the loss of separation with an airplane, vehicle or pedestrian.

2. Takeoff /landing without clearance.

3. Simultaneous takeoff and landing from the same or from intersecting runways.

4. Takeoff /landing from/onto the wrong runway.

A review of Air Traffic Management related accidents worldwide from 1980 to 2001 by the National Aerospace Laboratory in Netherlands found that 68% of the accidents involving Air Traffic Management occurred during the ground phase of flight.

There is a runway incursion every three or four days in Europe. There is a near collision due to runway incursion every three or four months in Europe.

Runway incursions occur in daytime as well as at night, in good as well as low visibility conditions.

Automatic Dependent Surveillance Broadcast

There are two new technological concepts that are now becoming a reality, which will greatly improve runway safety. One is a high tech solution and the other one is very low tech. After several false starts with other technology, the Federal Aviation Administration in the United States and other governments and their aviation regulation agencies are getting closer to implementing the Automatic Dependent Surveillance Broadcast system. This is part of the Next Generation (NextGen) aviation improvement system that the FAA is leading in the United States. They are coordinating this effort with the European authorities, which they call Single European Sky. There are many facets in the NextGen plan including software programs that improve precision approaches, help to merge airborne aircraft into a stream of landing aircraft, provide more direct approaches to an airport with Optimized Profile Descent as well as operational, technological and policy changes which will lead to shorter delays on the ground.

The Automatic Dependent Surveillance-Broadcast system uses the Global Position Satellite (GPS) system, which has very precise accuracy, to locate an aircraft on the ground and in the air. Three orbiting satellites provide the triangulation data that accurately identifies the precise location of an aircraft. The location of the aircraft on the ground is shown on a moving map display of the airport. Upon landing the pilot will switch from air mode to ground mode on the ADS-B system which will automatically display all of the runways and taxiways of that airport. Every aircraft on the ground is shown on the display and the pilots aircraft (own aircraft) is identified as a circle with an "X" in it. With this system the pilot or flight crew know exactly where they are on the ground and they can "see" every other aircraft around them. This system is better and faster than radar. Radar is dependent on a revolving antenna to send and receive a signal. Each revolution takes 4 seconds to complete. The ADS-B system refreshes data every two seconds, so it is twice as fast and is more accurate than radar.

Here are the details of what it is and how the system works. The Automatic Dependent Surveillance-Broadcast system is a surveillance system that relies on aircraft or airport vehicles to broadcast their identity, position and other information derived from onboard systems. This signal can be captured for surveillance purposes on the ground (ADS-B Out) or on board other aircraft (ADS-B In). The latter will enable airborne traffic situational awareness, spacing between aircraft and separation. One of the pluses for this system is that it is totally automatic.

The ADS-B system is automatic because no external stimulus is required. The system is dependent because it relies on onboard systems to provide surveillance information to other parties. The data is then broadcast. The originating source, like an aircraft, has no knowledge of who receives the data and there is no interrogation or two way contact.

The ADS-B system is a key enabler of the future Air Traffic Management Network, which is a key part of the Single European Sky in Europe and the Next Generation (NextGen) system in the United States. The vision for ground surveillance is en route and terminal area safety so controllers and pilots can see the runways, taxiways and other aircraft that are on the ground as well as other aircraft in the air. This is vitally important as the current ground radar systems may have "blind spots" in which the radar cannot "see" or get a reliable pulse return from a specific geographical location on the airport grounds. This very problem resulted in a fatal accident in Los Angeles on Feb. 1, 1999 in which a Skywest Metroliner turboprop was cleared to taxi onto an active runway while a U.S. Airways 737 jetliner was about to land on the same runway. The ground controllers could not visually see the gates and taxiway in question and thought the taxiing aircraft was on a taxiway. There were several problems that the ground controllers were handling at the time. The landing aircraft crushed the turboprop, exited the runway and slammed into a building. All 12 people on the Skywest aircraft died as well as 23 of 89 people on the U.S. Airways aircraft. The airport installed video cameras after the accident to provide the controllers with visual coverage of that blind spot. The ADS-B system will resolve that problem as GPS satellites can see everything.

ADS-B Ground Mode will work with other systems already in use, including Wide Area Multilateration or WAM. WAM is an independent, cooperative surveillance technology based on the same time difference of arrival principals that are used on an airport surface. WAM is a technique where several ground receiving stations listen to signals transmitted from an aircraft and then mathematically calculate its position in two dimensions. Altitude data is provided by the aircraft. That data is then fed into an automated air traffic control system which is displayed on an air traffic controller's screen. Airborne ADS-B systems will enable new separation modes in the air.

The upgrade in cockpit equipment will be fairly easy. Most commercial and business aircraft electronic systems are in a modular box that plugs in to a receptacle in the cockpit display systems. That makes repairs and calibrations quick and simple. The electronic boxes are repaired/calibrated in a lab setting on or offsite from the airport. Calibrated boxes are installed and tested by aviation technicians to verify that the systems are operating correctly and accurately.

For airports, a locally optimized mix of available technologies and ADS-B will provide an integrated airport operation. The air traffic controllers will be able to see everything that the pilots see. Eventually, this system will replace radar systems as ADS-B information is updated faster, every two seconds vs. four seconds with radar, and is more accurate. In the aircraft cockpit, this information is displayed on a moving map, when the aircraft is on the ground. Clouds and rain do not distort GPS signals whereas they do distort radar signals.

The Automatic Dependent Surveillance-Broadcast system will provide important features to the Air Traffic Management Network. The controllers will have surveillance everywhere on the ground with no gaps in coverage from gate to gate. This is an important step in the elimination of runway incursion accidents. They will also have full access to the air to air information in the sky, for complete air traffic situational awareness. Also, since ground based radar only works about 200 miles out from the transmitter, the new system will provide coverage over all of the oceans, including the most remote areas on this planet. The search for the missing Malaysia Airlines Flight MH 370 would have benefited greatly had this system been in place at the time of the aircraft's disappearance on March 8, 2014.

The new system will display all of the runways and taxiways of any airport. Then the system will overlay positions of all of the aircraft that are on the ground onto the airport runway map. Every aircraft and ground vehicle will be displayed as a circle with information identifying the vehicle, its position and direction. The host aircraft will be designated by a circle with an X in it so the flight crew knows exactly where they are on the ground and they can see every other vehicle.

The need for the new Automatic Dependent Surveillance-Broadcast system was demonstrated again in October of 2014. A business jet was cleared for takeoff at Moscow's Vonukvo Airport late at night and collided with a snowplow. The Dassault Falcon 50 was owned by Total SA oil company and carried the CEO of Total, Christophe de Margerie. Three French crew members and the CEO died in the crash. They were returning to Paris. An ongoing investigation is looking into the actions of the snowplow driver and the controllers. The ADS-B system would have shown the snowplows (there were three of them working as a team) with their position on or near the runway. This is a tragic loss for the French oil company as well as the people of Russia.

Some of the other benefits of the ADS-B system will be high performance, improved safety, increased capacity, cost efficiency as the system is cheaper than radar, more efficient flight profiles because controllers can see aircraft everywhere, and fuel savings. That leads to less air pollution which benefits everybody. ADS-B is being implemented in Europe, North America, Asia and Australia, starting in 2014 and will be complete by January 1, 2020. All aircraft will be required to have this system installed by then including all privately owned general aviation aircraft. One of the estimates I have read about the cost to equip or convert a commercial jetliner to the ADS-B system is $100,000 USD. However, once the conversion process is fully implemented that cost is expected to drop significantly. The cost for GA aircraft will be much lower than that. There are concerns in print that there will not be enough qualified electronic technicians in the general aviation field to implement this change/additional equipment. Time will tell. However, the current administrator of the FAA has stated that the deadline of January 1, 2020, is a firm completion date. Any aircraft without this equipment installed will be denied permission to taxi out for takeoff.

Two high tech avionics companies are in the forefront of the ADS-B development and implementation in North America. Honeywell and Rockwell-Collins have products on the market now that will handle ADS-B information. Honeywell has two software programs which are forerunners to the ADS-B system. Honeywells' SmartRunway software package offers an upgrade to existing software and is the first program on the market to provide pilots a visual real time prediction of runway performance based on the aircrafts expected acceleration or deceleration, weight, braking action, reported runway conditions and other factors. Their other software package, SmartLanding, provides too high, too fast, unstable and long landing information callouts if the aircraft's energy state is too high for the length of the runway. That information provides an alert for the pilots to initiate a go around. If the aircraft lands anyway, the system provides distance remaining callouts. This software would have made a big difference in the outcome of the American Airlines 737 landing accident in Kingston, Jamaica, in 2009. (There is more information about this accident in the Aircraft Interior Safety section of this book.) Neither of these software upgrades provides information on the position of other aircraft on the ground. That is where ADS-B comes in.

Prior to ADS-B research, both Honeywell and Rockwell Collins developed "Equivalent Visual Operations", an element of the FAA's Next Generation Air Transport System. EVO refers to the use of onboard synthetic and enhanced vision technologies to allow pilots to make visual precision landings when visibility and clouds approach zero miles horizontally and zero feet vertically. The aviation software industry continues to develop standards for the systems. Honeywell is favoring the placement of key information on the primary flight display while Rockwell-Collins is opting for similar cues on the heads up display. Both of these systems are evolving into the ADS-B system, which will provide more information to pilots without requiring extra infrastructure and training as part of a surface movement guidance and control system. The system shows the runways and the intersecting taxiways. The pilots would know where they are on the ground. However, they would not see other aircraft that are also on the ground. That will change with the ADS-B system. That new system will provide a huge increase in aviation safety on the ground. The Canary Islands accident is a big driver to get this new navigation system implemented.

Runway Status Lights

A low tech solution to runway incursions is a system of Stop/Go lights on the runways and taxiways. If a runway or taxiway is occupied by an aircraft or a ground vehicle the light turns red and the pilots/drivers know to stop. With a green light the pilots can continue to taxi to their destination. The lights are imbedded in the runway/taxiway. The system alerts pilots and drivers when it is not safe to enter, cross or begin takeoff on any taxiway or runway.

Los Angeles International Airport (LAX) was the third airport in the U.S. to test the prototype Runway Status Lights (RWSL) system which was designed by MIT Lincoln Laboratory, ARCON Corp., and the FAA. The system is designed to help reduce and prevent runway incursions and accidents. RWSL is a fully automatic, advisory safety system which operates independent of air traffic control using airport surveillance data from the ASDE-X radar system and advanced safety logic. The system calculates the future path of a vehicle and the possibility of a conflict. A traffic light will turn red to automatically stop a vehicle from intersecting another vehicle. The system is comprised of two sets of lights, runway entrance lights (REL) and takeoff hold lights (THL).

In Los Angeles the ADSE-X radar is connected to the Runway Status Light System along four runways and eight taxiways and is designed to detect potential collisions between two aircraft or an aircraft and a vehicle. The lights will turn red to alert pilots if the radar detects a potential conflict. This system is an additional enhancement to the Ground Traffic Control System. The controllers are still responsible for the movement of all vehicles on the ground.

Following Dallas/Fort Worth and San Diego, LAX is the third airport in the United States to use the system, which is installed and maintained by the Federal Aviation Administration. LAX has had the most runway safety violations in the United States for much of the 1990s but that number of incursions has declined from 21 in 2007 to five in 2009. The automated Runway Entrance Light system is designed to lower that further.

The FAA has developed the system to maturity and will install it at 17 other airports in the U.S. by the end of 2017. The Runway Status Light system is a low tech system that has proven its ability to reduce the incidence of runway incursions. This system is another forerunner of the ADS-B system, which was discussed earlier. The Runway Status Light system will be an enhancement to the new Automatic Dependent Surveillance-Broadcast system.

Rapid Exit Taxiway

Another runway safety feature that is starting to make its appearance is a change in runway layout. Most exits from an active runway are at a right angle to the runway. The landing aircraft has to slow down to 15 knots or so to make a 90 degree turn off the runway. The new design consists of a parallel runway that starts halfway down the active runway. The exit is called a Rapid Exit Taxiway (RET). The angle off the active runway to the rapid exit taxiway is shallow, perhaps 30 degrees, to allow the aircraft to exit at a high speed of perhaps 80 knots, after landing at about 120 knots. This gets the landing aircraft off the runway sooner which enables another aircraft to take off sooner than before. The aircraft that just landed will taxi onto the RET then taxi all the way to the end of the RET before crossing the end of the parallel runway, if there is one and it is safe to do so.

With a faster exit from the runway, more aircraft can land and takeoff. That is called a movement. With more movements per hour there is less wait time on the taxiway to take off, which reduces fuel consumption and air pollution. This runway enhancement is already being used in Mumbai, India, and Gatwick Airport near London, England. The RET in Mumbai has increased the number of movements from 48 to 50 per hour. UK's Gatwick airport, which has the busiest single runway operation in the world, now handles 55 movements per hour. That airport also has the best network of RET's and regular taxiways.

Here are the details of the Rapid Exit Taxiway system. The RET's are taxiways linked to runways at an angle that permits aircraft to exit the runway at high speeds (40–58 mph or 65–93 km/h). The intersection angle of such taxiways should not be less than 25° nor greater than 45°. Ideally, it should be 30°. These taxiways should include a straight distance after the turnoff curve sufficient for a landing aircraft to come to a full stop clear of any intersecting runway.

Runway Safety Council

In the fall of 2008 the Federal Aviation Administration in the United States convened its Runway Safety Council for the first time. It is a new joint government-industry body chartered to literally tear down the current runway safety culture and take a deep, systemic approach to improving runway safety and move toward a proactive management strategy that involves different segments of the aviation industry.

The council includes representatives from the FAA, the National Air Traffic Controllers Association, the Professional Aviation Safety Specialists, the Airline Pilots Association, the Air Transport Association, the American Association of Airport Executives, the Airports Council International, the Aircraft Owners and Pilots Association, the National Association of Flight Instructors, the National Business Aircraft Association and the Air Taxi Association.

The FAA believes a coordinated, systemic approach is necessary because serious runway incursions are seldom caused by a single factor. The existing safety culture separates responsibility for incursions into discrete categories: operational errors by controllers, pilot deviations and vehicle or pedestrian deviations. Investigations into incidents are currently conducted by different parts of the FAA, depending on the category of the incident.

The FAA intends the council to play a lead role in resolving critical surface safety issues with participating entities, dedicating resources such as subject matter experts and analysts, to a team that will examine the root causes of runway incursions. The Runway Safety Councils' Root Cause Analysis Team will investigate incidents from a systems perspective, getting input from airports, operators and air traffic controllers.

One focus of the council will be on how human factors contribute to runway incursions and what can be done to reduce human errors. The Root Cause Analysis Team will analyze and attempt to resolve issues in a positive, non-punitive environment. The team will recommend to the council ways to resolve or mitigate system risks. If the council supports the recommendations, it will work with different parts of the FAA to address what needs to be done, and track progress toward a solution of the problem.

The most current Runway Safety Council report I found online was the Runway Safety Report which posted data from 2011 and 2012. Below is the statement of the Vice President of the Runway Safety Council, Joseph Teixeira.

"Safety is the Federal Aviation Administration's number one priority. With our comprehensive Safety Management System (SMS), we now anticipate and correct risks before they jeopardize safety. By bringing attention to the potential hazards associated with the presence of aircraft, vehicles, and pedestrians in the runway surface environment, the FAA proactively improves flight safety.

"Our SMS provides us with a wealth of information, which, when compiled and analyzed, can give us a more panoramic view of our system, using a wider variety of data and a more holistic view of all the factors that contribute to safety. By blending the strength of our people, new technology, and enhanced analysis and procedures, we are seeing continued improvements in safety.

"There are four key elements to our safety strategy: collect and value information from our front line employees; deploy technology to gather relevant data; analyze and identify risk; and, finally, take corrective action that removes risk from the National Airspace System (NAS).

"Runway safety is everyone's business. The Runway Safety Council works with airlines, industry, pilot groups, and FAA lines of business to mitigate serious hazards on the runway. Working with all stakeholders, the FAA has developed innovative programs and techniques to reduce the number and severity of surface incidents, including implementing the international standard phraseology "line up and wait" and requiring explicit taxi instructions for runway crossings.

"The FAA conducts Runway Safety Action Team meetings at every towered airport in the country. In April 2010, we created the FAA's Airport Construction Advisory Council (ACAC) to increase awareness of closures and construction at various airports across the nation. Risk analysis greatly improves when stakeholders constantly focus on the runway environment.

"Our efforts also include comprehensive outreach, education, and training. These initiatives focus on keeping surface safety awareness at the highest possible levels among pilots, controllers, and vehicle drivers.

"This Runway Safety Report provides an overview of FY 2011 and FY 2012. It offers a comprehensive accounting of the accomplishments within the FAA, which is reflected in the associated runway safety metrics contained in this report. A review of the historic data highlights the significant progress made by the FAA in improving airport surface safety. We are fully aware that there will continually be new challenges to address.

"We are proud of our accomplishments to date, and remain committed to lead the effort to reduce risk associated with runway operations within the NAS. We will continue to work with our partners to develop new and innovative ways to improve runway safety in an ever-changing environment."

Note the creation of a subgroup, the Airport Construction Advisory Council. Their job is to make airport users aware of airport construction and taxiway/runway closures. This is a pretty big deal. On October 31, 2000, a Singapore Airlines 747, taxiing out for takeoff at night, in heavy rain from an approaching typhoon, turned on to a closed runway in Taipei, Taiwan, and collided with construction equipment. The aircraft, that was not quite airborne, crashed back onto the runway and burned. There were 79 fatalities among the 159 passengers and four fatalities among the 20 crew members on board the aircraft. The cockpit crew apparently did not look at the Primary Flight Display, as that would have alerted the crew that they were on a closed runway. This was a totally preventable accident. This accident, and others like it, may have driven the decision by the Runway Safety Council to create the Airport Construction Advisory Council. The information created by this group does save lives and prevent injuries.

It is reassuring to know that dedicated professionals are actively involved in activities that are designed to improve runway safety. For complete information about the goals and data collection about runway safety the reader can search "Runway Safety Council" online. I found data for my nearest local airport, Charles M. Shultz Sonoma County Airport. (Mr. Shultz was a longtime resident of Santa Rosa, California, and was the cartoonist who created the Peanuts cartoon strips. He, his wife and their adult son were/are pilots and agreed to rename the airport after Charles' death in February 2000.)

The report lists four runway incursions at my local airport during this report period. There are no details of those incursions in this report but it is a clear indication of how safe it is to operate aircraft on the ground there. This airport is considered to be a regional airport as it hosts general aviation aircraft, business aircraft, both propeller and jet, law enforcement and medical emergency aircraft as well as commercial passenger turboprop aircraft operated by Horizon Air, a subsidiary of Alaska Airlines. I have flown out of this airport twice with that airline.

The FAA's push to enable future airport operations in practically zero visibility is spurring a great deal of technology, not only for the airborne segment, but the ground portion of a flight as well. The concept is to use sensors and displays to give pilots a clear view of their path from the gate to the runway and vice versa. Ideally, that presentation will also include alerts for situations where there is the threat of an incursion from another aircraft or vehicle. This is where the new ADS-B system will contribute greatly to aviation safety.

European aviation authorities are also very active in all factors of runway safety. They are very aware that the worst runway incursion accident occurred within their sphere of influence. Runway safety embraces all matters concerned with the identification and prevention of hazards that might impede the safe take off, taxiing and landing at an airport of all types of aircraft. Runway Safety includes Runway Incursion and Runway Excursion.

The European Action Plan for the Prevention of Runway Incursions is based upon the International Civil Aviation Organization (ICAO) Standards and Recommended Practices (SARPs) and is therefore suitable for universal application. The ICAO Runway Incursion definition is "Any occurrence at an aerodrome involving the incorrect presence of an aircraft, vehicle or person on the protected area of a surface designated for the landing and taking off of aircraft."

Since the first release of the European Action Plan for the Prevention of Runway Incursions, Local Runway Safety Teams have been established at hundreds of airports across Europe. The implementation of the recommendations contained in the first version of the Action Plan has been extensive, thanks to these teams and the organizations that support them. The European Aviation Safety Agency (EASA) has now embedded this concept as an essential requirement to the European Union, "EASA Basic Regulation", and is a key element in helping to raise the issue of safety of runway operations at European airports. This is the European version of the Runway Safety Council in the United States.

Taxiing Aircraft

I have developed information about the Runway Alert and Advisory System (RAAS). This system has only been installed at a few large airports in the United States including San Francisco International (SFO). The RAAS sends an audio message to the cockpit when the aircraft is approaching a taxiway or a runway. The system does not alert the pilots about the presence of another aircraft but verifies their location on the airport.

A friend of mine, Edgar Beltran, is an aircraft technician for Alaska Airlines at Oakland International Airport (OAK) in Oakland, California. Edgar, and his wife Susie, live in a condo next to Ballena Isle Marina, where I keep my sailboat, JAMAICA 3. As an AT, Edgar is licensed, with an additional endorsement and training, by the FAA and Alaska Airlines to taxi empty jetliners around the airport. He has experience at San Francisco International (SFO) and Seattle/Tacoma (SEA) airport, as well as Oakland (OAK). He is among a handful of techs who taxi aircraft between the hanger(s) and a gate at a terminal. The airlines quickly found that it is much more cost effective to have aircraft technicians taxi aircraft around the airport than to pay pilots to do that job.

In a short interview, I asked Edgar about the Runway Alert and Advisory System. Edgar said that in clear weather the RAAS audio announcement is a bit of a surprise, as he can clearly see where he is on the airport grounds. But, in fog, at night or poor weather conditions, the RAAS system is helpful in verifying where an aircraft is located. However, its usefulness has been, or will be, surpassed by The Automatic Dependent Surveillance-Broadcast (ADS-B) system. ADS-B is a far more capable system.

That interview led me to ask Edgar Beltran further questions about training for that type of work. It's fairly simple. A Federal Aviation Administration (FAA) Ground Controller will provide training to any airline or vendor employee who has a need to drive a ground vehicle, like a catering truck, or an aircraft, around the airport. The first set of training is radio communication protocol and procedure. Then the drivers are trained to provide four items of information to the ground controller. The ground controller needs to know who the person is, where they are, what vehicle they are driving and where they want to go. With that information the driver will be directed to follow a specific route following markings on the pavement near the terminal. Aircraft that are taxiing have the right of way so trucks will have to wait for aircraft to clear the truck's path. Aircraft that are in taxi mode between the gates and a hangar provide the same information to the ground controller. The technician is then provided with directions to use specific taxiways and is monitored by the controller until the aircraft has reached its destination.

I received some more information about taxiing aircraft around an airport from a good friend, former member of Ballena Bay Yacht Club in Alameda, and lead mechanic for Alaska Airlines, now in Seattle, Mike Smalley. Mike used to work with/report to Edgar Beltran in Oakland. Mike writes:

"Each airline is different. They have their own rules and training procedures. I've worked at some airlines that wouldn't let a mechanic run and taxi (run only).

"At Alaska Airlines there is a multi-step procedure, and I believe you need not only a recommend, but a need to do so. In other words, somebody from the sheet metal or interior shop would not have a need to taxi aircraft.

"Once a need has been determined, there are a couple of classes that are required: 1) to be proficient in the type of aircraft and 2) the run and taxi training, which can take a period of time. Then you are passed off to another instructor for evaluation. Once you have been qualified to run and taxi, there is a 10 hour recurrent training class every two years.

"Here in Seattle (SEATAC) there is another caveat, which is that once a year we need to be recertified by the airport to operate a vehicle, i.e. an aircraft, on the 'movement area' of the taxiways and runways. This is to make sure we know how to read the signs, follow instructions from the tower (ground controllers) talk on the radio, etc."

This is exactly the information I was seeking. Now we know that the people who taxi commercial aircraft around an airport are trained and certified by the airline and the FAA to perform this task in a safe manner.

Following Instructions

Here is an example of what can happen when flight crews do not follow or understand instructions from the ground traffic controllers. I do not have all of the important details of who said what but this is the initial report of what happened. This runway incursion accident occurred in Johannesburg, South Africa, on December 23, 2013, around midnight, local time.

A British Airways 747-400 aircraft was cleared for takeoff on Runway 03L. The South African Civil Aviation Authority confirmed that the air crew received the correct instructions from the Air Traffic Control to taxi to that runway, 03L, using taxiway B. "The crew left taxiway B and continued onto taxiway M which is narrower, resulting in the aircraft impacting a two story brick office building." While looking at a Google satellite photo of the airport, I could see that the taxiway the 747 was on, taxiway B, curves to the left and ends at Runway 03L. The accident aircraft continued in a straight line, which becomes Taxiway M and leads to a general aviation area. Just after entering Taxiway M there is a two story brick building on the right side of the taxiway. General aviation aircraft and even business jets would have no trouble getting past that building. But a 747 can't clear it.

The right wingtip of the British Airways 747 collided with the building. Four people who were in that building were injured by falling debris. The 17 Crew and 185 passengers who were onboard the aircraft escaped unharmed and were evacuated from the aircraft through door number five.

It was reported that there was an indication of fuel spillage from the aircraft but this was contained by the airport fire services without further incident. South Africa Civil Aviation Authority investigators were dispatched to the airport that evening and the next morning where they witnessed the recovery of the aircraft as well as the removal of the flight recorder from the aircraft. British Airways cooperated with the agency in the investigation. The aircraft was moved to a remote site at the airport where airframe technicians repaired the damaged wingtip.

Here are the details. The aircraft involved in this accident was a Boeing 747-400, registration G-BNLL, performing flight BA-34 from Johannesburg, South Africa to Heathrow airport, London, England with 182 passengers and 17 crew. The aircraft was taxiing for departure and had been cleared to taxi to the holding point for runway 03L, via taxiway B, but missed the left turn towards runway 03L and continued straight onto general aviation taxiway M. The right wingtip of the 747, which has a wing span of 211 feet (64 meters), sliced into a two story brick office building next to taxiway M. Four ground staff of the cabin cleaning company Bidvest Group Ltd. were in the building and received minor injuries from falling debris while no one onboard the 747 were injured. The passengers and crew evacuated the aircraft via a mobile stairway. "This wasn't just a case of the wing grazing the building, this was a huge incursion," said Robert Mann, a consultant who formerly ran fleet management at American Airlines and who describes the London-Johannesburg route as a "senior route" which was most likely staffed by experienced cockpit crews.

A fuel spill from the fully fueled jumbo jetliner, which would have had thousands of gallons of fuel in its wing tanks, was contained by the airport fire services. That indicates to me that the fuel tank distribution network was not damaged by the impact. No one aboard the aircraft was injured, according to airport officials. The 747 was removed from the office building, towed to a remote spot in the airport and its flight recorders recovered for analysis. The passengers were taken to a hotel for the night and rebooked on other flights the next day.

I had the impression from the early news reports that the wingtip was repaired and the plane flew to London the next day. That was not the case. Apparently, further inspection of the accident aircraft revealed more damage than first thought. It is somewhat common for a jetliner to impact the wingtip of an adjacent aircraft when arriving or departing from a gate at a terminal. The force on the wing is relatively small and the damage is contained in the wingtip. The airplanes more or less bounce off of each other. The Airframe and Power Plant technicians call this type of damage "ramp rash". The technicians are called to the scene and can replace the damaged aluminum and light fixtures fairly quickly.

Now compare the force of a typical "ramp rash" wingtip to wingtip collision with the force exhibited in the Johannesburg runway incursion. The wingtip contacted an immovable object, the two-story brick building, while the weight (mass) and speed (slow) of the 747, exerted a great deal of force on the wing of the aircraft. The exterior of the wingtip was obviously damaged but other damage probably occurred in the wing and at the wing/body join point. In the center section of the fuselage, under the floor, there is a huge square structure called the wing box. The forward and aft sections of the fuselage bolt on to that structure, front and back. Each of the wings bolt on to the same structure, on the left and right side. The wing box is extremely rigid yet fairly lightweight. If the wing box was torqued or bent by the impact with the building then the wing would no longer be mounted in the correct position. That would impact the flying qualities of the aircraft, essentially grounding the aircraft. Also, if the plane was flown in that condition the wing box could collapse and cause a catastrophic accident. The cost of replacing the wing box is probably far greater than the value of the aircraft. At that point, the next move is a no brainer. Scrap the aircraft. Also, the parts of the aircraft could be worth more than the flying aircraft. That would include all four engines and the airborne power unit (generator) as well as the cockpit instruments and the interior of the cabin. The bare hulk can be sold as scrap to make new aluminum. In addition to that, British Airways announced some time before the accident that they planned to eliminate all of their 747's from their fleet by the end of 2016. They must have realized what other carriers have noted which is that it is more efficient to operate a large twin engine jetliner like the Boeing 777 or the Airbus A330 instead of a four engine Boeing 747. The fuel costs are lower while maintenance costs are 50% lower because of parts and labor for two engines instead of four. Plus, look at the load factor of this flight. (Load factor is the percentage of occupied seats on a flight.) This flight had 182 passengers and 17 crew on board. This model of the Boeing 747 can carry 450 to 480 passengers so that plane was only half full, or a load factor of around 50%. No airline can make money that way. All of those people would easily fit into a 777-300ER (extended range) or in Boeing's new 787.

One of the passengers took some photos of the damage out of a window. Harriet Tolputt, Manager of Media for the international relief agency, Oxfam, was on the flight and posted pictures of the incident on Twitter. She wrote: "BA plane crashes into building at J Burg airport. No one injured only the pilot's pride ... Not impressed that first class passengers get off before premium economy during an emergency." She posted this photo on Twitter which was picked up by media around the world. She obviously knows how to communicate with masses of people.

Crew Resource Management

It is possible that the runway incursion accident in Johannesburg, South Africa, could have been prevented had the non-driving pilot noticed that they had departed the assigned taxiway. One or both of the pilots did not notice the sign that indicates that Taxiway B curves to the left while Taxiway M begins straight ahead. A transcript of the cockpit voice recording has not been released yet. I am sure that the pilots were trained in Crew Resource Management.

One of the big aviation safety improvements, Crew Resource Management, has been around now for some time. I mentioned this earlier in the book. In 1979, the Congress of the United States passed a bill that required the National Aeronautics and Space Administration (NASA) to develop a program which would require both pilots in a jetliner to listen to each other and accept criticism and suggestions. This program, called Cockpit Resource Management, was developed and implemented as a direct result of two aircraft accidents in the United States. On December 28, 1978, a United Airlines DC-8, operating as UA flight 173, ran out of fuel while the cockpit crew was troubleshooting a landing gear problem. The flight, from JFK in New York, was on final approach to Portland International Airport in Oregon when the cockpit crew noticed an anomaly with the landing gear. After an hour in a circle holding pattern the engines flamed out and the plane crash landed in a wooded suburb. Of the 189 people on board, two crew members and eight passengers died. Why did this accident happen? The plane crashed to the ground because it ran out of fuel. The crash occurred largely because the captain ignored repeated comments from the first officer and the flight engineer about their fuel situation. (I have a female friend who is a surviving flight attendant on that flight.)

Six years earlier, on December 29, 1972, a four month old Lockheed L-1011 operated by Eastern Airlines as flight 401, also flying from JFK International Airport in New York but to Miami, Florida, crashed into the Everglades north of Miami, Florida. The entire flight crew was also troubleshooting a landing gear light problem and failed to notice that the plane was losing altitude, because the autopilot had been accidently turned off. From the 2000 foot holding pattern the plane descended to the ground in three minutes. The crash landing resulted in 102 fatalities with 75 survivors. The entire flight crew focused on the light problem and failed to notice that the plane was gradually losing altitude. No one was flying the plane or monitoring the flight systems.

The National Transportation Safety Board issued a landmark recommendation to require Crew Resource Management training on June 7, 1979. This recommendation was written by an NTSB safety investigator, Dr. Alan Diehl, who is also an aviation psychologist. Dr. Diehl was assigned the task of investigating the Portland crash of 1978 and he found striking similarities between the actions by the cockpit crews in that accident, the Eastern Airlines L-1011 crash into the Everglades in December of 1972 and the runway collision between the KLM and Pan Am 747s in Tenerife in March of 1977. As we now know, the captain on KLM was stopped from taking off without clearance twice, first by the first officer and then again by the flight engineer. But just after that the KLM captain initiated a takeoff roll without clearance and collided with the Pan Am 747. Shortly after the NTSB report was released, NASA held a workshop on the subject and endorsed the training program. In 1981, United Airlines became the first airline to adopt the program.

Various airlines may have their own name for Crew Resource Management but the rules and training are all the same. It is a set of training procedures for use in environments where human error can have devastating effects. CRM focuses on interpersonal communication, leadership and decision making in the cockpit. Basically, in aviation, the flying pilot is required to accept input, suggestions and opinions from the non-flying pilot. This became even more critical as the 1990s saw the elimination of the flight engineers position from the cockpit. That position was automated in the new aircraft flight management system. This program is also taught to air traffic controllers, surgical medical teams, police officers and firefighters.

Runway Separation

The minimum clearance between parallel runways, if they are to be used simultaneously, in Instrument Flight Rules (IFR) conditions, is 4300 feet. IFR refers to poor visibility when the pilot is flying on instruments. However, for Visual Flight Rules (VFR), or clear visibility, the minimum separation between parallel runways is 700 feet. Otherwise, landing aircraft have to be staggered on final approach so they do not touch down at the same time. The parallel runways at San Francisco International Airport (SFO) are 750 feet apart and in clear weather aircraft land in a staggered approach on both runways. When fog closes in, which is often the case, especially in the summer, the airport can only use one runway at a time for landing aircraft, which reduces movements from 60 per hour to 30. SFO has two sets of runways which are perpendicular to each other. Landings occur on one set while takeoffs occur on the other set. It is quite interesting, as a passenger, waiting for takeoff, to look out the window and see aircraft on final approach, especially at night. Right after aircraft land and clear the end of the takeoff runway, we are on our way.

There have been discussions about adding another perpendicular set of runways at SFO and I have seen five alternative plans for the layout. The airport is built on landfill right next to San Francisco Bay and extends outward into the bay. The proposed new runways would be further out in the bay and the runway that would become the middle one would no longer be used. This proposal did not get very far beyond the proposal stage. The FAA made the original proposal in 1999 and did so because SFO has the second worst weather delay rate in the U.S., behind Newark, New Jersey. To state this in another way, the on time arrival rate for SFO in 2012 was 71%. The Newark and LaGuardia airports have a 77% on time arrival rate. No other airport in the U.S. is below 80%. The FAA proposal went nowhere and was shelved after the terror attacks in 2011, which decimated air travel levels in the United States.

Environmentalists have threatened to sue the authorities over this proposal because the proposed runway extension would even further decrease the size of the bay and impact cities south of the airport. The new runways would need 107 million cubic yards of mud and would pave two square miles of the bay. The cost of one new runway almost anywhere in the United States is close to one billion dollars so the plan to build two of them at one airport does not seem to be likely. In addition to the cost and environmental impact of the expansion, the agencies involved must also consider the cost to benefit ratio. The cost of the proposal is very high but what is the benefit? Does it improve safety beyond what already exists? Probably not. If aircraft were colliding with each other on final approach there would be a huge public outcry. But there have been no collisions on final at SFO so what would be the benefit of building new runways? The main benefit would be that aircraft could arrive on time. The cost for that benefit is enormous and it helps a very small portion of the population. That is why the plan is still on paper only.

Getting to the airport in San Francisco can be a challenge at times. I always ride an airport express bus from my home in the north bay town of Santa Rosa as it is so much easier with much less stress for me. The two hour drive is a pleasant way to travel. The San Francisco Bay area took action starting in 1957 to relieve roadway congestion around the bay by building a subway system that connects the east bay (Oakland) to the west bay (San Francisco). The system is the Bay Area Rapid Transit or BART subway. A tunnel was built under the bay that connects the two cities. The rest of the system was built above ground level except for the trans-bay tube and extends north and east of Oakland. A station is located near the Oakland Airport with a new BART connection between the two. Recently, BART was extended in San Francisco, south to San Francisco International Airport with a stop just outside a terminal there. That has provided a means for travelers to go between SFO to downtown San Francisco and the east bay quickly and efficiently. BART carried an average of 373,945 passengers on weekdays, 176,616 passengers on Saturdays and 119,247 passengers on Sundays during the month of January 2013. This system is now the fifth busiest commuter rail system in the United States. It is now (2015) being extended south from Oakland to San Jose, the capitol of Silicon Valley. Only a small portion of the daily commuters go to and from the airports.

Traffic Collision Avoidance System

On April 25, 2014, two Boeing 757's nearly collided in mid-air, over the Pacific Ocean, about 200 miles east of Hilo, Hawaii. United Airlines Flight 1205, which was headed east from Hilo to Los Angeles and a westbound US Airways jetliner approaching Hilo on the big island of Hawaii got very close to each other. According to published reports, the aircraft were flying at the same altitude, 12,000 feet, which was assigned to them by an air traffic controller. That part of the incident is currently under investigation by a joint task force from the National Transportation Safety Board (NTSB) and the Federal Aviation Agency (FAA).

The incident was brought to public attention when a passenger on the eastbound United Flight 1205 wrote a blog titled: "Two Weeks Ago, I Almost Died in the Deadliest Plane Crash Ever." Passenger Kevin Townsend described the feeling of being weightless when the United Airlines 757 descended 600 feet in 60 seconds. "I felt my body strain against my seatbelt," Townsend wrote. "Passengers around me screamed. There was a loud crash in the back—a coffee pot clattering to the floor and tumbling down the aisle. Our tray tables began rattling in unison as the 757 strained through the kind of maneuver meant more for a fighter jet."

Kevin Townsend estimated that both aircraft carried a combined total of about 590 people. He wrote that had they collided, the death toll would have surpassed the worst aviation accident in world history, the Canary Islands accident. Both aircraft in this incident were equipped with the Traffic Collision Avoidance System.

I have not found any information about what happened on board the westbound US Airways jet but thanks to United Airlines passenger Kevin Townsend we have a clear indication of what it was like for the people onboard the United Airlines aircraft.

What saved the aircraft from colliding? The two pilots in the United Airlines 757 received an audible warning from the Traffic Collision Avoidance System (TCAS). This system monitors the airspace around a plane and notifies the cockpit crew if there is a possibility of another plane coming close to it. How does it work? Here is a simplified explanation.

The traffic collision avoidance system, (TCAS) (pronounced tee kas) is an aircraft collision avoidance system designed to reduce the incidence of mid-air collisions between aircraft. The system monitors the airspace around an aircraft for other aircraft equipped with the same active transponder, which is independent of air traffic control, and warns pilots of the presence of other transponder equipped aircraft which may pose a threat of a mid-air collision. All aircraft that weigh more than 12,600 pounds or can carry more than 19 passengers must be equipped with TCAS. The system is based on secondary surveillance radar transponder signals, independent of ground based equipment, which will provide advice to the pilots about potential conflicts with other aircraft.

The TCAS system communicates automatically with other aircraft transponders. Each TCAS equipped aircraft interrogates all other aircraft within a predetermined range about their position (via the 1030 MHz radio frequency) and all other aircraft reply to interrogation (via 1090 MHz). The interrogation and response cycle may occur several times per second. The system automatically reads the direction, speed and altitude of other aircraft and calculates if there is a threat of an intersecting path. TCAS is only able to interact with other aircraft that have a correctly operating mode C or mode S transponder. A unique 24-bit identifier is assigned to each aircraft that has a transponder. A protected volume of airspace surrounds each TCAS equipped aircraft. The size of the protected volume depends on the altitude, speed, and heading of the aircraft involved in the encounter.

The next step the TCAS system performs, after identifying a potential collision, is automatically negotiating a mutual avoidance maneuver (currently, maneuvers are restricted to changes in altitude or modification of climb/sink rates) between the two (or more) conflicting aircraft. These avoidance maneuvers are communicated to the flight crew by a cockpit display and by synthesized voice instructions.

There are two types of warnings. The low threat level warning is a Traffic Alert or "Traffic", meaning that an intruder is near, both horizontally and vertically. The Required Action is to attempt visual contact and be prepared to maneuver if a resolution advisory occurs.

The other type of warning is more severe and intense. Those are called Resolution Advisories. With a RA the system mandates IMMEDIATE evasive action. For instance, if the audio warning is "Climb: Climb" the required action by the pilots is to climb at a rate of 1500 to 2000 feet per minute. The approaching aircraft will pass below the aircraft taking evasive action. There are twelve possible required actions in the TCAS system but only one traffic alert. After the conflict has passed, another message is heard which is CC or Clear of Conflict. That means that the intruder is no longer a threat and the pilots can return to their assigned altitude, or promptly return to their previous ATC clearance.

Passenger Kevin Townsend further reported that after the near collision off Hawaii in April 2014, the lead flight attendant, or purser, came on the intercom and apologized for the hardship and panic caused by the sudden maneuver. About 45 minutes later the pilot made a more detailed announcement. I imagine the pilots took that time to verify what had happened with air traffic control and per-haps take a lavatory break! I am sure the encounter was very intense.

Near mid-air collisions are fairly rare and actual mid-air collisions are very rare but they have happened. In 2002, there was a tragic mid-air collision over southern Germany which made a huge impact on the public of Russia and their President, Vladamir Putin. A Russian built jetliner collided with an American freighter with no survivors. I had the impression that the Russian-made Tupelov jetliner did not have TCAS in its cockpit. That was not the case and this is what happened.

On July 1, 2002, near midnight, Bashkirian Airlines Flight 2937 flying from Moscow, Russia to Barcelona, Spain, collided with DHL Flight 611, a freighter, over the towns of Uberlingen and Owingen in southern Germany. The Russian built aircraft was a Tupolev Tu-154M passenger jet carrying 60 passengers, mostly children, and nine crew. The DHL aircraft was a Boeing 757-23APF cargo jet manned by two pilots. The DHL flight originated in Bahrain but was on a leg from Bergamo, Italy to Brussels, Belgium. That indicates the Bashkirian flight was head-ing west while the DHL flight was headed north. The planes were flying under the supervision of Swiss air traffic control at the time of the collision.

Both aircraft were flying at 36,000 feet (FL 360) and were on an intersecting course. The private Swiss airspace control company, Skyguide, was controlling the flights from Zurich, Switzerland. The controller, who was working on two radar workstations at the time, failed to realize the problem in time to keep the aircraft at a safe distance from each other. At just under 60 seconds prior to the collision the controller realized the problem and contacted Bashkirian Airlines Flight 2937, instructing the Russian pilots to descend a thousand feet to avoid the crossing traffic, DHL Flight 611. As the Russian crew initiated their descent, their Traffic Collision Avoidance System (TCAS) instructed them to climb. At the same time the TCAS system on DHL Flight 611 instructed them to descend. The Russian crew, unsure about which instructions to follow, continued their descent and eight seconds later the planes collided. The vertical stabilizer of the DHL sliced through the Bashkirian airliner just ahead of the wing. The forward fuselage of Flight BA 2937 fell away to the ground while the remaining part of the fuselage continued in flight briefly before it too plummeted to the ground. The DHL Flight 611 struggled for another four miles without most of its vertical stabilizer before it too fell to the ground. There were no survivors. It is widely believed that had the Russian pilots followed the TCAS instructions the collision probably would have been avoided.

This tragedy did not end on the ground in southern Germany. Two years later, the controller who was handling the flights was stabbed to death by a man who lost his wife and two children in the accident. I think it is important to remember that people operate aircraft and other people do their best to observe and control aircraft from the ground. We need to remember them. Peter Nielsen was the controller on duty that fateful night in 2002. He was attacked, stabbed and died outside his home in Kloten, near Zurich, Switzerland. His killer in the February 24, 2004, attack was Vitaly Kaloyev, an architect. He was arrested, tried and convicted of the murder in 2005. After two years in prison he was released after an appeal which found that his mental state at the time of the murder was not sufficiently considered in the initial sentence. After his release from prison in Switzerland he moved to North Ossetia, which was part of the Republic of Georgia. In 2008 he was appointed deputy construction minister of that country. Bashkortostan is northeast of North Ossetia.

The Russian aircraft, Bashkirian Flight 2937, was piloted by an experienced crew. Captain Alexander Mihailovich Gross, 54, led the cockpit crew. His copilot was First Officer Oleg Pavlovich Grigoriev, 40. The pilot had more than 12,000 flight hours of experience. Grigoriev, who was the chief pilot of Bashkirian Airlines, had 8500 hours of flight experience and his task on this flight was to evaluate Captain Gross' performance throughout the flight. Joining them on this flight was a pilot who was normally the First Officer, Murat Ahatovich Itkulov, 41, a seasoned pilot with 7900 flight hours. He did not officially serve on the flight crew due to the captain's assessment by the chief pilot. Also in the cockpit was Navigator Sergei Kharlov, 50, with 13,000 flight hours and Flight Engineer Oleg Valeev, 37, with almost 4200 flight hours of experience.

The DHL cargo aircraft, operating as DHL flight 611, had originated in Bahrain and was piloted by two Bahrainian based pilots. British Captain Paul Phillips, 47, with 12,000 flight hours of experience and Canadian First Officer Brant Campioni, 34, with 6500 flight hours.

Bashkirian Airlines Flight 2937 was a chartered flight from Moscow, Russia to Barcelona, Spain. Forty-five of the sixty passengers on board were Russian school children from the city of Ufa, the capital of Bashkortostan, who were on a school trip organized by the local UNESCO committee. One of the children's father served in that organization and most of the other parents of the children were high ranking officials in Bashkortostan. The country is a federal subject in southwestern Russia, located between the Ural Mountains and the Volga River.

The TCAS software package works very well. In the collision known as the Uberlingen Collision, the system designed to keep aircraft separated in the sky did respond to the threat but human error inserted conflicting information. That led to a fatal delay in action by the Russian pilots.

A business aviation pilot friend of mine, Steve Campbell, has told me that this accident has been studied extensively by aviation and regulatory authorities, on multiple continents, looking for a missing link in the aviation system that allowed this accident to occur. (Steve has a commercial, multi-engine and instrument rating and is the lead pilot for a commercial real estate firm in San Francisco. He commutes to his office in a high rise office building on the San Francisco waterfront from Ballena Isle Marina in Alameda aboard a small, rugged, enclosed power boat. The company plane is a Beech King Air, a twin engine turboprop.) The authorities in Germany and Switzerland did identify several problems that led to this tragedy and have taken steps to sharply reduce the possibility of this type of accident. In May of 2004, the German Federal Bureau of Accident Investigation published its report about this accident, as they had the jurisdiction. They determined that the accident had been caused by shortcomings in the Swiss air traffic control system, which was supervising the flights at the time and by ambiguities in the use of TCAS. Part of the technical problems in play at the time of the accident is that the prime radar system was down for maintenance but the controller was not informed about this change. The controller was looking at the backup radar system which was not as fast as the normally operating system. In addition to that, the radio system was being serviced as well so the controller was using an older, slower system. Investigation showed that the maintenance crew failed to communicate with the controller to inform him of which system was operating at the time. That misled the controller, who believed that he had plenty of time to resolve the conflicting flight paths.

In addition to that, the pilots' manual for the Tupelov 154M includes a statement that reads "For the avoidance of in-flight collisions is the visual control of the situation in the airspace by the crew and the correct execution of all instructions issued by the Air Traffic Controller to be viewed as the most important tool. TCAS is an additional instrument which ensures the timely determination of oncoming traffic, the classification of the risk and, if necessary, planning of and advice for a vertical avoidance manoeuver." That means that the pilots are instructed to obey ATC instructions over TCAS instructions. (The quote is most likely an English translation of the Russian instructions.) Also, at the time of the accident in 2002, there was no downlink of TCAS instructions to the controller, so they can see that a Resolution Advisory had been issued and what that advisory was. That automatic downlink had not been deployed worldwide yet. There were additional circumstances as well that led to this tragedy. I encourage the reader to search for and read the complete report online.

I feel that there is a connection between this collision in the sky over southern Germany and the collision on the ground in Tenerife. The KLM 747 that ran into us was carrying around two hundred children, who were with their families, travelling to a vacation spot on the Spanish island of Grand Canary Island. The Bashkirian Airlines flight was carrying a special group of forty-five older children, who had high academic achievements in their local school system, to the Spanish city of Barcelona. All of these children did not get the chance to become leaders or contributors in their local communities. We will never know what they might have become.

Extended Twin Operation

Prior to 1985, most jet aircraft flying long distance over open water were three and four engine aircraft, starting with the Douglas DC-8 and the Boeing 707, progressing in the late 1970s with the three engine McDonnell-Douglas DC-10 and the Lockheed L-1011 and the four engine Boeing 747. When the aircraft manufacturers and the airlines began to propose the use of twin engine aircraft for long haul flights over water the FAA began to look at establishing rules for the use of that type of aircraft operating under those circumstances. The FAA issued rules in 1985 that govern the flying time a twin engine airliner, prop or jet, can fly from the nearest landing site. That is the diversion time rule which is the flying time to the nearest approved airport. That could be over land or water. The initial diversion time rule for jets was 180 minutes, which means that at any time during any given flight, the aircraft must be able to fly to an approved airport within 180 minutes while flying on a SINGLE engine. This is called Extended-range Twin Operations or ETOPS.

Any new passenger twin engine aircraft model has to be ETOPS certified by the manufacturer. The certification is based on the actual flying ability of the aircraft, which has to be proven to fly reasonably well for an extended period of time on one engine. The jet engine manufacturers and the airlines have gathered data which proves that jet engines in use today have a very low failure rate which results in a very high reliability rating. This has allowed airlines, for instance, to fly from the west coast of the mainland United States over the Pacific Ocean to the Hawaiian Islands, which is about a five hour flight from San Francisco, to use twin engine jetliners instead of three or four engine aircraft. Even longer flights are available today. United Airlines operates a flight from San Francisco to Shanghai, China, with a Boeing 777-200ER. Operating those types of aircraft provide the airlines with a better operating profit margin because those aircraft use less fuel and require maintenance on only two engines. ETOPS rules have evolved over recent time to the extent that some aircraft may be certified for more than 180 minutes because of proven reliability of the jet engines. This rule benefits everybody on the planet because twin engine aircraft use less fuel which results in less air pollution.

On August 5, 2014, the ETOPS rule made an appearance in the international news media. A nearly new Boeing 787 lost power in one engine while over the Atlantic Ocean. The British holiday charter carrier, Thomson Airways, operating flight TOM 157 from Santo Domingo, Dominican Republic, to Manchester, England, with a Boeing 787-8 Dreamliner, experienced an engine anomaly more than halfway into the nine hour flight. The captain decided to shut down the right engine, after an oil pressure warning light came on, and then decided to divert to the next alternative airport, which was the Azores Islands. Immediately after the engine was shut down, the plane descended from 41,000 feet to 23,000 feet to get to a lower altitude which has higher air density. The higher air density was needed to provide sufficient lift under the wings. The flight was 450 nautical miles west of the Azores at the time of the emergency. The plane, one of six 787-8s owned by Thomson Airways, made a safe emergency landing at the military airbase in Azores Islands, a possession of Portugal, about ninety minutes after the right engine was shut down.

I have learned that an accessory gearbox associated with the right engine on the 787-8 failed to maintain proper oil pressure. The captain decided to shut the engine down to avoid the risk of serious engine damage caused by the lack of lubricating oil. This type of failure is fairly common in the jet engine industry but this is the first inflight failure of the General Electric GEnx-1B engine. In March 2014 a Japan Airlines 787 made an emergency landing in Honolulu, Hawaii, also because of low oil pressure in one engine. The flight was on a Tokyo to San Francisco route when the captain diverted to Honolulu. There was no information about the manufacturer of that engine. (GE also makes the larger GEnx-2B engine that powers the Boeing 747-8 Intercontinental jet.) The first Boeing 787-8 was delivered to a customer in the fall of 2011. Thomson Airways was Boeing's United Kingdom launch customer and received its first of six 787-8s in June of 2013, thirteen months before this incident.

The joint Portuguese/American Lajes Airbase is on the island of Terceira, Azores. (In 1976 the island chain became officially known as the Autonomous Region of the Azores.) This military airbase has a small commercial terminal that handles scheduled and chartered flights within the Azores Island chain as well as flights among Europe, North America and Africa. The 288 passengers on board were asked to stay on the plane, because of overcrowding in the terminal at the time, as they waited for a replacement aircraft. The cabin crew restocked the aircraft and provided food and drinks for the passengers. Shortly after that, the passengers were welcomed aboard a Thomson 767 aircraft that flew down from England to pick them up. The passengers arrived at their destination about 11 hours late, but they were safe.

The Azores airbase has been there for a long time. The nine inhabited volcanic islands in this chain are in the mid-east Atlantic Ocean, about 850 miles west of continental Portugal and about 550 miles northwest of the island of Madeira. (Madeira is also a Portuguese island. I visited there on a port of call on the repeat Mediterranean cruise in 1978 as a passenger aboard the Golden Odyssey.) The island chain extends for 370 miles in a southeast to northwest orientation. In 1944, the American armed forces constructed a small and short-lived air base on the island of Santa Maria, which is in the southwest part of this island chain. A year later, a new base was constructed on the bigger island of Terceira. The air base is in an area called Lajes, a broad, flat sea terrace that had been a large farm. Lajes Field is on a plateau rising out of the sea on the northeast corner of the island.

Lajes Field continues to support the American and Portuguese armed forces. During the Cold War, U.S. Navy P3 Orion antisubmarine patrol aircraft flew over the North Atlantic Ocean from this airbase, on the hunt for Soviet Navy submarines and surface warships. Since its opening, Lajes Field has also been used as a refueling stop for American military aircraft bound for Europe, Africa, and the Middle East. The U.S. Navy keeps a small squadron of its ships at the harbor of Praia da Vitória, three kilometers southeast of Lajes Field. About 1200 military personnel are assigned to the base while the island chain has about 50,000 inhabitants.

Twin engine long haul aircraft like the Boeing 777 and the Airbus 330 have been joined by the new Boeing 787 Dreamliner to provide passengers with a comfortable ride on a long flight. In the summer/fall of 2014 more airlines announced that they are removing Boeing 747s from service and replacing them with heavy twin engine aircraft. Boeing's order book for the venerable 747 is very bleak and Airbus is having trouble finding customers for the huge double decker A380. Airlines around the world have realized that the economics of large four engine aircraft do not make sense in today's market. Large twin engine airliners are leading the way to profitability for the airlines. And all of those aircraft are ETOPS certified.

ᰍ   Chapter 26   ᰍ

CONCLUSION

As you have become aware, there are many aspects of runway safety. Collisions on the ground account for 63% of all aircraft accidents in the United States. That is why there is so much effort to reduce that threat. Many government and industry groups on several continents are actively involved in developing equipment and procedures to decrease the possibility of runway incursions. I believe that the development and implementation of The Automatic Dependent Surveillance-Broadcast system will greatly improve situational awareness on the grounds of any airport. The cockpit crew can readily see where they are on the ground and see where all the other moving aircraft and ground vehicles are located. When this system is fully implemented, I am confident the flying public will have a much better chance of arriving at their destination unscathed.

In addition to The Automatic Dependent Surveillance-Broadcast (ADS-B) system, which will be a huge improvement in situational awareness, especially on the ground, airport management teams are installing equipment and modifying taxiways to make movements on the ground safer and faster. The installation of runway traffic lights does keep aircraft and ground vehicles from entering or crossing occupied taxiways and runways. In addition to safety on the ground, these improvements reduce traffic delays, which, in turn, reduce fuel consumption and greenhouse gas emissions.

As electronic and digital technology have improved, so have aircraft control systems. A recent improvement in aviation ground safety is the digital transmission of messages from the ground traffic controllers to the flight deck. This is like an email which provides details of an aircraft's departure path. These messages provide the ground taxi route information and separately provide departure information, which is called Clearance Delivery. There are a limited number of departure flight paths out of any airport. The controller choses the path that best guides the aircraft to its destination. This automation does reduce the noise and possible confusion in the tower and the cockpit which improves situational awareness and concentration while reducing repetitive messages. The controller chooses the taxi path and departure clearance with its digital message and sends it to the aircraft, as identified by its flight number.

In addition to ground runway safety, I pointed out one of the major airborne safety enhancements as well. The Traffic Collision Avoidance System (TCAS) scans a broad space around the aircraft looking for other aircraft that might intersect its flight path. It then warns pilots of danger or instructs pilots to commence evasive action.

Jet engine technology has advanced to the point where an in-flight failure of an engine is a very rare occurrence. Even if an engine fails on a twin engine aircraft the plane will fly well enough to get to the nearest approved airport. The in-flight shut down rate of jet engines in the 1960s was 40 times per 100,000 flight hours. Today the rate is less than one. In other words, in the 1960s an average jet engine would fail once a year. Today, on average, a jet engine fails once every thirty years. That is a huge improvement in reliability.

All of these enhancements are about people. Some people need to fly to meet with customers, which keeps their businesses prospering. Some people want to fly to visit with relatives or friends. Other people, like myself, want to fly to find out what it is like in another place on our planet. Those desires are the main driving force behind the aviation industry. Those desires create jobs for many people who manufacture aircraft parts, software, assemblies and complete aircraft. Those desires also create jobs for people who operate, maintain, regulate and secure aviation activities and provide services for travelers. All of those people help us go to, and return from, the places we need and want to visit.

Flying on a scheduled, commercial aircraft has never been safer than it is right now in 2015. Statistically, it is more dangerous to drive to and from the airport than it is to fly on a scheduled carrier anywhere in North America and Europe. Lawmakers will continue to push the regulators and industry to improve their safety records. And the flying public will continue to ask for further improvements in safety.

June 15, 2009
By Roger Yu, *USA Today*

Wikipedia–ADS-B

Honeywell Corporation, Phoenix, Arizona

June 15, 2009
By Roger Yu, *USA Today*

Airport Check-in: New LAX radar cuts runway incursions
June 15, 2009
By Roger Yu, *USA Today*

Data analysis by Andrew Bailey

Joseph Teixeira
Vice President, Safety and Technical Training
Air Traffic Organization, Federal Aviation Administration
CNN

SKY News

By Kevin Crowley and Andrea Rothman, *Bloomberg News*

Simon Hradecky, *Aviation Herald*

Martin Blanc – *Bidness ETC*

Paul Ausick – 24/7 Wall Street
Charlotte Cox – *Mirror*

James Durston – CNN Travel

Wikipedia – BART

Wikipedia – Uberlingen Mid-air Collision

Steven Gomez – Honeywell Aerospace

David Timothy – Honeywell Aerospace

RT-News – Moscow crash

Telegraph.co.uk – Moscow crash

ABOUT THE AUTHOR

Before his retirement, David Alexander worked in microwave technology for companies such as Teledyne MEC, the division of Hewlett Packard that became Agilent Technologies and for JDSU. His passions always have been music, travel and boating on the San Francisco Bay. At age 29, he survived the world's deadliest plane crash on his way to his second cruise vacation, the first on the Mediterranean. He has refused to live in fear and since the incursion has built himself a satisfying life that includes volunteer work, lots of time sailing on his Jamaica 3 sailboat berthed in Alameda, California, and international vacations. This is his first book. He lives in Santa Rosa, California.

If you would like to contact the author, please email him at: neverwait.firetruck@gmail.com or look for David Alexander on Facebook.

ABOUT THE COVER PHOTOGRAPH

The image on the book cover is one of five images I shot after I escaped from the burning Pan Am 747 wreckage. Pan Am Clipper Victor was not burning this badly when I jumped off the wing between the two engines and ran away from the plane. After a gas explosion from the left wingtip, the entire plane caught on fire. I ran farther away, then stopped and documented what I saw with my camera. The engine closest to the camera, engine number one, continued to run after impact until the fan blades knocked off the engine cowling. I found the woman on the wing right over the inboard engine. The exit door over the wing was pushed out at the top by the deformed fuselage. I was sitting one row in front of that door. To the right of that door, the fuselage sloped downward in a jagged edge. This is where the KLM 747, City of Amsterdam, crossed over us and sheared off the whole back end of our plane, separating the vertical stabilizer from the fuselage. The people standing in the left foreground are co-survivors. I don't know who the man on the left of the trio is but the other two are Patricia Daniel (middle) and her daughter Lynda.

Printed in Great Britain
by Amazon

33125202R00096